Post Pardon Me

A fickle woman's spiral into postpartum **depression and anxiety and how the hell she found** her way out of it. *(Sort of.)*

SUZANNE YATIM ASLAM

This book is a memoir, based on a mix of personal recollection and historical fact.
The author has tried to recreate events, locales and conversations from memories
of them. For reasons of discretion, in some instances the author may have changed
the names of individuals and places. They may also have changed some identifying
characteristics and details such as physical properties, occupations and places of
residence.

To Kasim, my good karma.
To Sammy and Ronan, you light up the world.
To the Mothers—you are more incredible than you know.

PART ONE

JUNE 10, 2014:
THE DECISION

The air felt weird. It was a mixture of tension, nervousness, and excitement. I was like a child—and children are in no position to even have this type of conversation, let alone make an actual decision about it.

Yet here we were, pretending to be adults, discussing, in my opinion, the most adult topic one can discuss with her husband. And just like so many other subjects, our points of view differed.

"Just think of all the money we'd save if we didn't have kids," Kasim said. "What about all the time we wouldn't have? Think of today—this morning we spontaneously decided to beat the heat and leave Phoenix for the day and bam...road trip to Sedona. We couldn't do that if we had kids."

"Yeah, that's true," I replied hesitantly. I was confused. Two weeks into the two of us dating, Kasim asked me what I thought our kids would look like. Yet now, my husband was trying to talk me out of it. I thought he always wanted this. It's strange that after almost five years together we're not on the same page here.

The truth is I have no idea if I want to be a mother. I think I just always assumed it would happen. It's what everyone does. But does that mean I actually want it? Why doesn't someone tell me what I want? I have no idea how I am supposed to make this monumental decision.

We kept walking through Sedona's main tourist trap area as I let my mind work, mulling over his words and my own thoughts.

Then it hit me. The foolproof argument.

"Here's what I think," I began slowly. "I don't think people regret having children, but I do think they can regret not having them. And when we're fifty and there's no chance of having kids of our own, will we regret it?"

The smartest man I've ever met didn't respond instantaneously as is his nature. He looked to the left of the street and allowed himself to be distracted by the giant flamingo-pink Jeep convertibles, stuffed with tourists who clearly didn't want the bother of enjoying nature and walking through red mountains. It seems they would rather be driven, inhaling the fumes, while the tour guides showed them all the natural healing energy vortexes that fill this city. The irony was not lost on me.

We walked around quietly, both of us taking in what I had just said. This trump card I had just played had only now occurred to me and I too needed time to digest my own words.

Right on cue, in an award-winning performance, the actors took their places and began the show. Families with children appeared out of nowhere: a mother was dragging her two small boys out of a Native American jewelry store yelling something about how she told them they're not supposed to touch anything; a hot dad was wearing a contraption that allowed him to carry his sleeping baby girl (with a hair bow bigger than her face) on his chest; grandparents were walking down the street with their teenage grandkids asking them where they'd like to go for dinner. I couldn't have planned it better. God has quite a sense of humor.

I noticed Kasim was looking at all of this too, but he never said anything so I just watched him watch them. As we turned right and made our way up the street toward our dinner destination he said, "Alright, let's do it. Let's have a baby." I thought I was going to throw up. Never in my life have I been so nervous. I didn't respond right away. I wasn't capable.

We walked in silence for a few minutes. I'm sure Kasim expected a response at some point, but I think it was his turn now to digest his own words and he seemed too lost in his own thoughts to mind the pregnant pause.

Night seemed to be creeping up on us. I've never really liked making decisions at night. It's as if the lack of light makes its way into my thoughts, darkening my clarity.

The lull could go on no longer. "Are you serious?" I asked as we walked across the small gravel parking lot. The string lights that hung along the front of the restaurant had just turned on and seemed to be greeting us, beckoning us inside for some classic sushi. "You're right," he said as he swung open the door and let me in. "We'll probably regret it if we don't."

And with that final point solidified, we were greeted by a hostess. We effortlessly turned on smiles and carefree demeanors and followed her through the empty restaurant to a small table for two in the corner that looked out onto the street. We sat down, opened up our menus, and thanked her as if nothing important had just happened—as if we hadn't just made the biggest decision of our lives.

JUNE 20, 2014:
THE PAIN

Sometimes I really hate being a woman. Having periods is already a nightmare. I know we're all used to it, but honestly, to bleed profusely once a month starting at age thirteen is just ridiculous. I think evolution screwed up somewhere because this makes no sense. Was there no alternative? If we decided not to have a child could we opt out of this whole thing?

My ovulation isn't any better. This week we meant to start trying, but I couldn't let him touch me. Another fail point of evolution: If the part of my cycle when I ovulate is the time I am supposed to accept a man's sperm, then why on God's green and blue earth would I be in so much pain? Why would it be so painful to even lift my leg up to put on pants? See what I mean about evolution messing up?

Apparently I suffer from a condition with a delightfully delicate little name called Mittelschmerz. It doesn't really mean anything other than "it hurts when you ovulate."

I suppose we'll try again next month. I'm frustrated. If they got rid of all the endometriosis, then why does it still hurt? The doctors can't find anything else wrong with me. My mom says having a baby will make it all go away. That pushing out the baby also flushes out whatever else is going on in there. Frankly, I find that to be appalling. I shan't be the one to tell my child that she was essentially the equivalent of an Aspirin.

People seem so casual about having kids. They seem to do it for weird reasons or no reason at all. Isn't this something that merits a little thought? I can't think of any decision bigger than this one, but because every single person before us has done it, it's just looked at as so normal, a "go with the flow" sort of thing.

Sometimes I worry that I can't get pregnant. There are hundreds and hundreds of stories about how the scarring that endometriosis creates in the uterus makes it difficult to conceive. Given that I have no idea if I actually want a baby, I wonder how I would feel if it turns out that I can't have one. I'm not sure I'm willing to go through alternative routes if my heart is barely in it. That doesn't make sense to me. Alas, I have yet to find that wise old sage who is supposed to tell me what I want. Man, this is the shit they don't prepare you for in school: how to pay taxes, whether or not to pay insurance on a rental car, and how to decide to have a kid.

JULY 13TH, 2014:
WE HAVE LIFTOFF

Well, I've done it. We've done it. Well, we've done what we can. My ovulation pain was manageable this month, so we tried.

I like that this has become the phrase we collectively use. "Yes, Baba, we're trying to have a baby." Not that we told anyone, but it's just weird to think of telling your dad about all the sex you're having in order to give him a grandchild. Am I thinking too much about this? Of course. But this is who I am. And it's bloody exhausting.

Waiting is weird. Right now, as I'm writing this, a million little tadpole-looking things are making their way through the lower half of my torso, dying off, a few thousand at a time, until eventually one last little guy, who apparently never has to stop for directions, hones in on my egg who is so elegantly waiting there for him.

I can see it now: there she is, the egg, looking very coy as she casually, accidentally on purpose (like so many women), reveals a bit more leg than she intended, making the zooming tadpole stop so quickly in his tracks that a puff of smoke comes up behind him. He looks at her, a smile lining just one side of his face. He runs a hand through his fuzz and in the cockiest manner, makes his way over to her and drops the cheesiest of lines.

"Hi. I'm sorry to disturb you. I don't usually do this, but when I saw you, I just couldn't take my eyes off of you."

"You're not disturbing me," she might say while playfully touching his arm, waiting to see if that spark is there, that bolt of electricity one feels when two people touch for the first time and they know there's something special there.

I'm convinced this is how it happens.

I know it's sort of cliche to talk about how it's a miracle, but when I really think about it, it is. What are the chances that this happens so smoothly so many times for so many people? Perhaps evolution has a few things figured out.

JULY 31ST, 2014:
HAPPY BIRTHDAY, HARRY POTTER

Today was a perfectly normal day. I went to the grocery store after work to pick up ingredients for dinner...and a pregnancy test. The girl working the checkout happened to be one of the neighbors in our apartment building. She bagged up my stuff, eyed me with a smile, then wished me good luck. Man, that really bothered me. One can assume that the good luck she was bestowing upon me was her assuming I wanted my test to come out positive. But what if I didn't want to have a baby? What if I grabbed the pregnancy test because I noticed I was late and this was the last thing I wanted? And here she was, as sweet as can be, wishing me good luck. Get out of here.

I know I've thought about this "good luck" more than she has, it just makes me wonder; we're always so quick to assume having a baby is a good thing, but what if it's not? What if you're someone who had a terrible childhood and you haven't worked through it yet? What if you're not financially ready? What if deep down you have no desire to have that kind of responsibility and you somehow end up resenting the kid?

We're past all that wondering.

As I was preparing dinner, I drank a lot of water and waited for the need to go pee on a stick. Halfway through chopping up the vegetables, the need arose. I grabbed the First Response box and strolled over to the little half bath by the kitchen. I peed on the stick, left it in the bathroom, and waited outside the door for what would naturally be the longest three minutes of my life.

Positive. It was positive. It happened. But I wasn't going to run upstairs just yet to tell Kasim, who was working away. I didn't want it to be a false positive. I guess that's why they always provide two tests. So I chugged some more water and continued chopping with butterflies and nerves growing ever stronger.

Now I was experiencing the longest twenty minutes of my life, waiting for the need to pee on stick #2. The moment arrived. I repeated the process diligently, making sure to do it right; to quote Rachel from *Friends* when Phoebe asked her if she peed on it right, "How many ways are there to do that?"

Positive.

I walked back into the kitchen and arranged all the food into the baking dish and put it into the oven. I set my timer, as I was sure my mind would be on other things—and the last thing we needed was a fire—and proceeded upstairs to share the news.

"Hey," I began, trying and failing to be cool as a cucumber. Kasim turned around in his swivel chair. "What's up?"

I sat down on his lap, kissed him, then I pulled the most recent test from my pocket.

"Oh my God," he said as he pulled me in for a hug. We just held each other for a while, not speaking. After what felt like a fortnight because cuddling isn't my forte, he pulled back and looked at me. He let out a sort of exasperated breath and then a laugh. It was a strange laugh. I had never heard a sound like that escape his lips. It was a bit of a crazed laugh, if I had to describe it.

"Dinner smells good." Of all the things to say right now, this is what he decided the moment called for. Honestly. I smiled and laughed, surprising myself with that same crazed sound Kasim had just made a moment before. Perhaps it's contagious.

"Who should we tell and when?" I asked, eager to keep the topic on track.

"Let's call my mom first since she doesn't live here, and the rest of the family we can tell in person. But we'll do all that tomorrow," he said.

I smiled and nodded. "I have to finish dinner. I'll let you know when it's ready." I kissed him once more and headed downstairs to the kitchen to continue my task.

When dinner was ready, Kasim made his way downstairs and we sat down at the dinner table, grabbed the iPad (we don't have a TV) and watched *It's Always Sunny in Philadelphia*. Neither of us spoke. I sensed that same air that I did in Sedona, that cocktail of tension, nervousness, and excitement. *This is it. The moment we talked about has arrived.* Yet there we were, not talking about it.

"How's the roast?" I asked him. "Good," he replied, while

keeping his eyes on the tiny screen. I sat there, pushing my food around my plate but not really eating the good roast. I couldn't figure out how I was feeling. Yes, I had those anxious feelings, but I couldn't really pin down what that meant. I kept wondering what he was thinking, but I didn't know how to ask him. Maybe it's that I didn't want to know. I convinced him to have a baby while he was trying to talk me out of it. Then I realized what I was feeling: scared. Scared that my husband might be mad at me for essentially forcing this idea on him, this idea that is now a reality. I worried he would regret it and resent me. Even in the most important moments I find myself worried about what everyone else is feeling and thinking.

While I don't believe in fate, I did find out that I am pregnant on Harry Potter's birthday...maybe magic is real.

AUGUST 1, 2014:
DRUNKEN MONSOON

I am exhausted. What a weird day. This morning we woke up around the same time and we just looked at each other, both of us with our eyes somewhat bulging out of our heads. The sinking realization of parenthood was kicking in. There's a baby in my belly. A baby that I am tasked to take care of. Kasim had two people to look after now. I knew he was thinking this without him ever uttering a word.

A couple of days after we got married, knowing we wanted to save our money and not go on a honeymoon, we headed two hours north, right past Sedona, to a little college town called Flagstaff. At one point, while going for a walk, I looked over at Kasim, who had been quiet for some time. Rather than looking out at the beautiful scenery filled with wood cabins and pine trees (something so vastly different from Phoenix that you can't help but to be in awe of it), he was staring at the sidewalk with his brow furrowed in deep contemplation.

"What's wrong?" I asked him, in the hopes that he would say nothing was wrong. We'd only been married three days, what could possibly be wrong?

"I have to take care of you now," he said, still not looking up from the sidewalk.

"What?" I replied.

"I have to take care of you now," he repeated as if I didn't hear him. That always drives me crazy about Kasim. When someone gives you news that you don't understand, it's typical to respond by asking "what?" It doesn't mean you didn't hear, it just means you didn't get it. And for some reason, he has never understood this. Oftentimes, his superior intellect leaves little room for some social norms. So I tried another path.

"What do you mean you have to take care of me now?" There. Clear as a bell.

"What do you mean what do I mean? I have to take care of you now. I have to make sure you're happy, that you're safe. I have to protect you."

Kasim had a difficult upbringing, fraught with insecurity. I knew the idea of protecting the people he loved meant a lot to him. I smiled and rubbed his back. "I'll take care of you too, habibi."

So here we were, this morning, lying in bed, and he had that same face. Now there are two of us for him to protect from this world—a charge he takes more seriously than any man I have ever known. I knew where his head would go if I didn't try to lighten the mood.

"Do you want to call your mom and tell her?" I asked Kasim. Today was just about sharing good news with our family.

"Sure. I'll go get my phone."

Naturally, there were tears during the phone call. Nancy is a crier. I don't do well with criers. What are you supposed to do while they're sobbing? It's weird.

We told her we hadn't told anyone and to keep it a secret for now. She replied with, "Well, I was thinking of moving back to Phoenix but now I absolutely have to!"

Thank God we were not on video call. Kasim and I looked at each other, slightly shocked, but I'm an actor and I'd like to think I'm a good one. "Oh my God, then the baby would have all four grandparents living here!" I'd like my Oscar now, please.

And there we have it. It looks like my mother-in-law is leaving the armpit of America that is Albuquerque (Kasim's words, not mine) and making her way to Phoenix. I've always been nervous about mothers-in-law. I haven't known very many that are actually good to their daughters-in-law. I guess I'll figure it out—or I'll be putting on a performance for the rest of my life.

Anyway, to get back to the topic at hand. It was a typical work day, so Kasim and I got up and dressed and headed downstairs to make breakfast. I love our breakfasts: fried eggs, sliced avocado and tomato, bacon for Kasim, toast, Irish cheese dipped in honey, a huge bowl of fruit, and, of course, coffee. As I was preparing food, I wondered how much time I would have to make big breakfasts when the baby was born. But I tossed that thought to the side. *I'm not yet ready to think about that.*

"Can we go tell my family tonight?" I asked while dipping cheese into some honey. They live about thirty minutes away, so it seems right to tell them in person.

"Of course," said Kasim. "The team and I are going to Salty Senorita after work for a meeting, but it shouldn't be long. I'll let you know."

When I went to work, I immediately called my bestie, Sofia, who lives in Chicago, and walked to the back corner of the rug store lest I be overheard by that nosey bookkeeper, Shelly. Honestly, she's worse than a one-upper. She likes to be the first to know everything so she can go around telling people as if this news has been confided directly to her as she is all supreme.

And true to form, when I walked back to my desk, Shelly looked right at me and said, "You're pregnant." She didn't ask, mind you. It was a statement. I work with my father-in-law and he was going to be in the store soon and I'll be damned if she told him first.

"Yeah, I'm pregnant. Don't say anything. It's still early," I replied in a sterile manner as I had no desire to be chummy with her. And since clearly there is no privacy to make a call, I texted Kasim instead and told him we had to tell his dad asap, explaining that some people have antennas for ears.

It's interesting how it will always unravel, a secret, that is. What's that saying? "Two of you can keep a secret if one of you is dead." For some reason, pregnancy secrets spread quicker than your average "I heard he's getting fired" secret or "she kissed a girl and she liked it" secret. Kasim said he'd stop by the store around the same time his father got in under the guise of wanting to talk about business things with his dad.

Saeed and Kasim walked into the rug store at the same time, their hair slightly messed up from the wind that seemed to be picking up outside.

"Good morning, Ami!" I said, addressing my father-in-law. "Hi, my love." I turned to Kasim and hugged him.

"Hey Pop, you got a minute to go next door and get some coffee?" Kasim, in all his coolness, asked Saeed.

"Sure," Saeed said, never being one to turn down a nice chat next door at Cafe Paris.

The three of us walked in, Kasim and I hand in hand, and found a table in the corner next to a poster of Mont Saint-Michel, the gorgeous abbey in northern France that I had the privilege of visiting as a teenager. I stared at the poster for a bit while the guys chatted about work stuff. Mont Saint-Michel is one of the most amazing places I have been to and looking at that picture of it, I began to imagine what it would be like to take my child there someday.

I imagined walking around the village that surrounds the abbey where the monks and nuns live. We would hear the sounds of the waves that surround the tidal island, crashing onto its temporary shores. We would find a small restaurant and eat locally caught oysters and mussels, making faces as we attempted to swallow the booger-like consistency. We would wash it down with sparkling water, bread, and cheese. Hand in hand, we would walk through the hallowed halls of the monastery that feels like a cave, hearing our voices echo, bouncing off the strong walls. We would talk about what it would be like to have a simple life, being one of the small group of inhabitants of the Mont Saint-Michel village. Our minds would wander, taking in every sound, every touch, every smell.

"Bonjour," said Caroline, the cafe owner as she walked up with menus and began handing them out, taking me out of my daydream.

"Bonjour," the three of us said in unison. "Could I get a latte with honey, please?" asked Kasim.

"Oh, that sounds great. I'll do that too," I said. "Decaf!" I added at the last second. "I already had a cup today. Don't want to be too jittery."

Saeed ordered a coffee, and Caroline left us to chat.

Kasim got us started. "Well, Pops, you're gonna be a grandfather." Man, he just got right to it.

I'll save you some time. There was a lot of "oh my God" and "I can't believe it" and "wow I'm so old now." You get the picture.

Caroline returned with our coffees, we all thanked her more enthusiastically than is normal, and we chatted away while enjoying our drinks.

Besides the snooping of Shelley the Spy, it was a lovely morning telling Kasim's parents our news. It's weird telling divorced parents something like that. Having a grandchild, I imagine, is a bit of a bonding experience. It must be weird to bond with someone you have been divorced from for twenty years.

Kasim went back to his work and I continued with mine. My sister, Selwa, kept calling me and I wouldn't answer because how the hell do I talk to her all normal when I haven't yet told her about the baby? She went from being my annoying baby sister to the person I tell everything to. And this was something that had to be told in person.

Saeed and I enjoyed our workday together, with this little secret between us, as we talked to clients. My father-in-law was kind enough to give me a job at his beautiful rug store last year. I've been struggling with work. I want to be an actor. I suppose you could say I am one, but it's not full-time work. Even with an agent, I can only get so many auditions and the competition is fierce. So I shoot the occasional indie film or commercial, but I'm not yet Angelina Jolie.

Really, I wanted more than one thing. I wanted to be a human rights activist and an actress. Hm, I guess I really do just want to be Angelina Jolie. After college, human rights work, the field I majored in, was hard to come by. (That's what happens when you graduate in the middle of a recession.) So I had a few jobs here and there, coffee shops, retail stores, but it was all horrible. That's when Saeed stepped in and offered me a job at his rug store, working in the Custom Rugs department, where I get to help rich clients design rugs. It's not too shabby. It's not my dream job, but Saeed is flexible should I need to go to an audition in the middle of the work day. Kasim, running his own digital marketing firm by day, has also been acting for years so his father understands our love for it.

Anyway, here's the good part.

I got home first and walked Milani. I asked my sister-in-law,

Fizza, if I could drop the dog off at her house tonight because we made plans to go to LA (more on that later). Kasim called me just as I was coming back in from walking the puppy.

"Hello?"

"Hello, my honey bunches of lovin' oats!" I could barely hear Kasim over the sound of loud music and drunk people at whatever bar he was in.

"Uh, hi?' I replied nervously.

"It turns out I am unable to drive myself anywhere. Could you come get me?"

"You're drunk?! It's 5:30, Kasim!" I yelled. This was the last thing I needed. And this is not like him at all. Kasim is more of a one glass of wine kinda guy. And he's beyond the peer pressure stage. This was weird.

"What? I got good news. I'm happy! I'm slightly nervous too, hence the need to be inebriated," he slurred.

"Oh Lord. Fine. Where are you again?" I asked as I started grabbing Milani's things to take to Fizza's.

"The Salty Senorita in Old Town."

"In OLD TOWN?!" I yelled. "But that's the OPPOSITE direction from my parents! And we still have to drop off Milani!"

"I'm sorry, my love. So when are you coming?"

"Ugh. I'm on the way. Hold tight." I finished grabbing Milani's and my things, threw her in the car, and set off to the other side of town mad as hell. Peoria, where my parents live, is thirty-five minutes away from us, and I was driving twenty-five minutes in the opposite direction to pick up my dumbass husband during rush hour traffic. I was bloody livid.

I pulled up to the front of the restaurant and called to tell him I had arrived. He came stumbling out the front doors. I've never seen anything like it. Kasim stayed awake long enough to listen to me yell at him about today of all days and whatnot and then passed out with the window rolled down. The wind was picking up even more now, but I'd rather that than keep the window up and smell the stale alcohol rolling off him.

I really struggle with my emotions, particularly my temper. Once I'm mad, it's nearly impossible to be anything else. I don't know how to just let it go and move on. I tried some deep breathing, thinking that the best thing I can do for my child is to find a way to stay calm. The breathing helped. So did the cool breeze that seemed to be keeping pace with my little Prius.

When we parked the car at Fizza's I very roughly woke him up. I may have calmed down, but I still had no desire to treat him nicely. We climbed the steps to the second-story apartment—well, I walked, Kasim crawled. Honestly, Milani was more composed than he was. Naturally, Kasim ran straight for the bathroom. While he was in there, there seemed to be confusion on Hassan and Fizza's part about why he was drunk, why I was this angry, and why I wanted to go to my parents' place now when clearly Kasim needed to go home.

"Fine, " I said, "I'll tell you guys. I'm pregnant." I didn't say it as enthusiastically as you'd think I would. But the prior event seemed to have deflated me.

Of course, they responded beautifully—a big bear hug from Kasim's brother, Hassan, and tears from my favorite and only sister-in-law, Fizza. She has a beautiful little daughter and now Aliyah was about to have a baby cousin. Fizza and I yapped away, bonded now by motherhood, as we waited for Kasim to get out of the bathroom. After a while, I got fed up with politely waiting and went to check on him. He seemed to only have made it halfway through the door. I found him passed out on the floor, the bottom half of his body still in the bathroom, his head and torso in the hallway. He wouldn't get up. He made a few grunting noises but that was all I could get out of him. I was fuming and crying. How were we going to go now? My family was waiting for us.

"Leave him here. I'll go with you," Fizza so sweetly said.

"I can't make you do that, Fizz," I said through sniffles.

"It looks like it's gonna rain. I'm not gonna send you to Peoria alone in the rain during monsoon season," she stated in her serious voice. I knew Fizza well enough to understand that was the end of the discussion. "Give me a few minutes to tell Hassan what to do for Aliyah. He can put her to sleep."

"Thank you, Fizz," I said quietly. She left me in the hallway and I stood there looking down at my husband on the floor, who, bless him, at the moment looked like a damned idiot.

I kissed Milani goodbye. I did not, however, kiss Kasim goodbye. Fizza and I got in my Prius and headed to Peoria. It helped to have a second person in the car—I could now use the HOV lane and avoid traffic a bit. It was getting dark pretty early, even though the sun usually didn't set for another couple of hours; the clouds were setting in and it smelled like rain was on the way. I love that smell. It reminds me of growing up in St. Louis. On rainy days, my mom would make herself a cup of coffee and me a warm cup of milk with a few drops of coffee and a teaspoon of sugar, and we would sit on the front porch swing and watch the rain fall as we waved to the cars driving by.

My phone rang. "Oh crap, it's Selwa. I'm already like an hour late," I said as Fizza took the phone away from me.

"Just drive," she said and she answered the phone. "Hello?" she said in a breezy voice.

"Uh, Suz?" I could hear my sister say through the phone.

"No, it's Fizza. Hey, Selwa!"

"Hi, Fizz! I'm confused. Where's Suz?" Selwa asked.

"Kasim got sick, but I needed to get out of the house so I came instead. We're on the way. We should be there soon," said Fizza assuredly. "Okay, bye!" She hung up before Selwa could say another word. At this point I just started laughing. This was all bananas and it was so hard to stay mad watching sweet Fizza attempt to lie.

Fizza joined me in laughter. Then the rain hit. "Oh shit," I said, "this doesn't look good."

We proceeded to laugh more. This day was just too much and there was nothing left to do but laugh.

Growing up in Tornado Alley, I know how to drive in the rain. I also know when it's stupid to keep driving. The rain was getting harder, to the point that I could no longer see the car in front of me, the wind so strong that my little fuel-efficient Prius couldn't handle it. We pulled over, put on our hazard lights, and waited it out.

"This is really nuts," I said to Fizza. "What a day. I can't believe Kasim. He's acting like an idiot."

"Eh, ease up on him. He just found out he's gonna be a dad. That's a big deal. And he doesn't have to be as put together as you since he's not carrying the baby. I'm sure if the situations were reversed and he was pregnant, you and I would be at the bar now celebrating."

I hate it when she's reasonable.

"Yeah. You're right. This isn't like him at all. I guess it's just hitting him hard and he needed to let loose a little," I said, really just thinking out loud, chewing on what Fizza so wisely said to me.

"The rain is letting up. Ready?" Fizza asked.

I nodded and pulled back onto the highway. We got to my parents' house by 9 p.m. Of course before I even got there, my family had guessed. As soon as I told them all and the crying stopped, Selwa broke down the series of events.

"I mean, why else would you show up this late, in a monsoon storm, with Kasim sick, unless you had something really important to tell us? And you've been married for three years so what else could it be?"

"Okay, okay, fine. But I couldn't wait another day to tell you."

Fizza and I stayed there for about an hour and then, full of happiness from the family and food from my mom, we headed for home. When we got back to her apartment, Kasim was still half in, half out of the bathroom, and Hassan was lying on the couch happily watching *Breaking Bad*.

At this point I was less angry than before and could see the humor in Kasim's appearance. I loved him so much at that moment. He must be so terrified to become a father, to shoulder that responsibility. I gently knelt down and rubbed his back.

"Habibi, wake up. It's time to go," I said in my softest voice. He mumbled something and slowly pulled himself up. Fizza appeared with a glass of water, handed it to me with a wink, and left us. Kasim drank the whole thing and rested his head against the wall.

"I'm gonna be a father," he said in a slightly confused manner.

"You're gonna be a great father. If you ever get up off this floor. Hassan and Fizza want to go to sleep. We need to go home, my love." He nodded and let me help him off the floor.

"Sorry we couldn't go to your parents' house tonight," said Kasim.

"What are you talking about? I did go. Fizza went with me."

"Huh? How long was I on the floor for?" he asked groggily.

"A few hours," I said and attempted not to roll my eyes.

"I'm sorry."

"It's okay. It was a big day for all of us," I said calmly. "Love you guys," I said, turning to Hassan and Fizza. "I'll call you when we're back in town." They bid us farewell and we went home.

Kasim is currently passed out and I should be too, really. I'm exhausted. And we're driving six hours to LA tomorrow. But I couldn't sleep just yet. I needed to wind down. So this is me winding down.

About going to LA: we're considering moving there. It's supposed to be where actors and writers go. It's where all our industry friends have moved. I have no idea what to expect. C'est la vie!

AUGUST 4, 2014:
LA IS A SHITSHOW

LA is a shitshow and I'm not raising my baby there, not even if they got rid of all the traffic. We spent two days talking to our actor friends and they all seemed sad and jaded and disenchanted. So thanks, but no thanks. K, bye.

AUGUST 21, 2014:
THE HIPPIE SPECTRUM

I drive a Prius, my major in college was International Human Rights, and I'm obsessed with fixing the environment. So it should come as no surprise at all that I want a home birth. Why bring a baby into the world in a place where people go when they're sick? And I can absolutely have it naturally—what with my terrible periods, ovulations, and endometriosis, I can handle the pain of childbirth. I'm a perfectly healthy young woman. There's no reason I shouldn't try it naturally like all my foremothers before me.

Yeah, Kasim wasn't enthusiastic about it.

"At home? That's a terrible idea. What year is this? Is it even clean enough here?"

"Yes, it's clean!" I yelled out defensively.

"I didn't mean it's dirty. Babies are just so sensitive. And what if you needed a C-section? Or the baby needed medical care?"

"I'd much rather give birth at home than where people go when they're sick. It's not like I'm going to give birth in a field. Midwives do this all the time. It's perfectly safe. And there are hospitals everywhere," I said, making a perfectly logical point.

Kasim weaved a pen through his fingers and thought about it.

I suppose it's his baby too and if birthing his child in a kiddie pool in our living room made him nervous then he's entitled to his opinion. But I'm nothing if not resourceful.

"Could we meet in the middle? I heard about these places called birth centers. It's all the comfort of giving birth in your home but in a bit more of a controlled environment with equipment at hand for emergencies."

"Let me do some Googling first. Then let's at least check them out," he replied.

I acquiesced to his need to Google everything. And while he did that I set up a few appointments at the best birth centers in the city, knowing that Google was going to tell him that my idea is bloody brilliant. Happily they were near each other so we spent an afternoon sightseeing the facilities.

I like to think of myself as a bit of a hippie—but it turns out there is a spectrum of hippiness, and the first birth center and I were on opposite ends of the scale.

We walked in and were greeted by a lovely woman probably in her forties. If you were to cast a midwife for a movie, this is who you would cast; she was draped in shawls even though it's August, she had bangles up and down both wrists, and she wore colors that I think you can only get away with in the Southwest: burnt orange, reds, and soft browns.

"Hello," she said in a soft, sort of dreamy voice as she shook our hands. "I'm Cindy. You must be Suzanne and Kaseem?"

Most people don't get his name right and most of the time, we don't even bother to correct them.

"Yes, that's us," I said as seriously as I possibly could, lest I break out in a stupid grin.

"Welcome to Baby Dream. Ready to get started on the tour?"

"Uh, sure, yeah. Let's do it."

She turned around gracefully and led us to the other side of the small building. There were two rooms for giving birth. One had a private bathroom inside of it, and the other room had a bathroom across the hall.

We smiled and nodded, taking in the information politely, but I knew it wasn't right. You know the feeling you get when you just know? Well, I just knew. I knew I would end up giving birth at the same time as someone else and she would get the room with the bathroom and I'd be stuck walking across the hall half naked every few minutes to use the loo. No, thank you. And it was as simple as that.

We said our thank you's, telling Cindy we would be in touch soon. We got into our car, ready to make our way to the next birth center.

Kasim spoke first. "That was weird."

"Yeah. I wasn't feeling it. God, I hope the next one is a bit better. Did you see those orange walls? I don't think that would help me stay calm while I push out a baby."

"Ready for the next one?" he asked.

"Sure," I said with a lack of enthusiasm as I pulled out my phone and mapped it. "It's just two miles away."

Five minutes later, we found ourselves at our second destination. I prayed this was it. I don't want to give birth at a hospital. I really think I can do this naturally if in the right environment.

We heard a little bell ring as we pulled open the door and stepped in. We found ourselves in a lobby greeted by a pleasant, clean scent. The lobby had gray walsl, a white sofa, and one small bookcase full of books that were all about the one topic these people specialize in. Hearing the sound of people ahead, we walked further in and turned the corner. We found ourselves in a cozy, open space, with women sitting in a circle, some sitting on the floor and some in chairs. They all seemed to be holding newborn babies and just chatting about motherhood. I won't lie, it was a bit uncomfortable seeing all those tiny creatures, some with poopy diapers, some crying/ screaming, some latched onto a woman's breast that was exposed so casually.

"Hello, can I help you?" A woman had just walked out of a room and into this open area where my husband and I stood, a bit out of our element.

"Hi, yes, I'm Suzanne. We have a tour scheduled."

"Yes, of course. Let me grab a folder for you, I'll be right back." She turned and walked into yet a different room. I watched her go. She didn't look like a midwife. I had only met the one midwife thus far, so my idea of what one looked like was very specific. This woman, however, had short, straight, slightly messy hair, and she was wearing a T-shirt with khaki shorts and Birkenstocks. This is why you can't stereotype people. You just never know.

Mercifully, she was back quickly with file in hand, and she escorted us into the first room. It looked like a regular examination room but with softer lighting and a small kiddie table and toys.

She sat down first in a single chair and gestured to us to sit on a couch opposite her, then handed us a packet to look at.

"Thanks for seeing us," I said.

"Of course. Congratulations. I'm Angela. Let me tell you a bit about myself. I'm an OB/Gyn but I've always had a soft spot for natural birth. In my previous life, I worked in a standard clinic, but I was discouraged with the system and I wanted a way to help mothers bring their children into the world without the entanglement of our current healthcare system. I have two children, two boys, both of whom I delivered with the help of a midwife. Any questions so far?"

I turned to look at Kasim, who hadn't said so much as a word since we walked in. If anyone was ever out of his element at any point in the history of civilization, it was this man, right now, in the midst of mothers and the babies that were birthed to said mothers naturally.

I looked at him and then back to Angela. "Uh, no. Not yet. We don't really know what to ask. I know I wanna try to have a natural birth. But I'm a little scared. I had endometriosis and I don't know if it's gone, so I don't know if that's going to affect anything."

At this point, she began a quick but strong lecture about the female body and its truly wondrous capabilities.

As she was wrapping up, there was a knock on the door. "Come in," Angela said.

In walked a woman who I recognized immediately as a midwife. She had long, black, curly hair, glasses that magnified her already large eyes, and a baby on her back that seemed to be held in place by a series of intricate ties and knots of a large scarf. She spoke in a dreamy voice, the kind of voice you want to hear when you're in an excruciating amount of pain as a baby is being pushed through the birthing canal.

"Hi, I'm Kathleen. I'm Angela's partner," she said, introducing herself, then she turned to Angela and said, "Hey, could you take the call on hold, it's Banner Health again."

"Sure," said Angela, getting up out of her seat. "Guys, I'm gonna let Kathleen take over from here to give you a tour of the facility. I need to talk with this insurance company. We've been playing phone tag." And with that, she walked right out of the room.

We stood up to greet Kathleen, who was walking toward us now with her arm extended.

"Who's the little one?" I asked.

"This is Henry, he's my youngest," she said in that light, fluttery voice.

"How many do you have, if you don't mind me asking?" Kasim asked. He finally spoke. I think by this time, he had gotten past being stunned by this whole operation and had moved on to the assimilation stage.

"I have eleven children," she said casually.

"ELEVEN?!" Kasim and I both said in horror.

"We're Catholic," she said with a chuckle. You could tell she was used to this response. "Would you like to see the birth rooms?"

We followed her back out into the main open room, past all the mamas and babies, and back into the front lobby. There was a door on the edge of the lobby that I didn't notice before. She walked up to it and put a code into the keypad and unlocked the door. She went in first and we followed her, staring at the back of Henry's head.

It was wonderful. Not his head, the rooms. Though he did have a cute little round head. There were two rooms, essentially two master suites with their own private bathrooms. Yes, that's right. No walking out of your room in your birthday suit and into a bathroom across the hall. So far, so good.

Each room had its own theme of sorts. The first room was called Peach Blossom. The walls were painted in a light peach color and there was an interesting stained glass window at the head of the bed with geometric shapes. Its bathroom was large and tan colored, with a fairly big tub.

The second room was called Cherry Blossom. Essentially it looked like the room you would get a massage in. It had slightly darker but still soft tones and no window.

I gave Kasim an approving look. He returned the sentiment.

Kathleen chatted with us, explaining how the birth center works.

"You'll see both of us, Angela and me, during your pregnancy, because we can't know who will be on call when you go into labor. You'll take turns seeing each of us at every other appointment. We recommend not having anyone come to your birth or even the birth center except for those that are part of your birth team. Your family and friends can visit you at home. Many women feel so much pressure and stress when they know their families are down the hall waiting for the birth of the baby. We don't want that for our mothers.

"Unlike at a hospital, we encourage you to eat. Labor is hard work and you need to be fueled. We don't want you eating a full meal, but it is important to have something. We have a full kitchen and we provide food for you, but if there's anything special you would like, you're welcome to bring whatever you want with you and keep it in the kitchen. After the baby is born, you can stay as long as you need to, we don't kick you out to make room for the next patient."

We finished up our tour with Kathleen and Henry and then said our goodbyes.

"Oh my God, I love it!" I said as we closed the doors to our car.

"Yeah, I do too," said Kasim. "It's across the street from the children's hospital, should there be any problems with the baby, and it's not far from St. Joe's in case you have any complications. And I like that they're so different—one being a traditional midwife and one being a doctor. It's the best of everything."

"So you're okay with this? Giving birth here?"

"Yeah, I think it's a great idea. Good job finding it, love bug," he said as we pulled out onto the main road.

I was relieved. We had found it, the place where our baby would be born. I made a mental note to call them in the morning and schedule my first official appointment.

So there you have it. A hippie dippie, badass, no-drugs birth. God, I hope I can do this.

SEPTEMBER 11, 2014:
WORLD PEACE DAY

Today was horrific.

Have I mentioned that my father-in-law wants to start a sort of religion? It's called Axiom. He wrote a book about it. I read it and I get where he's coming from. He talks about how he grew up Muslim in Pakistan, but then came here to America as a young adult and was exposed to other beliefs. He was dating a Christian girl and his best friend was Sikh. He admired them both for their strong beliefs in their faiths and the way they served their respective deities. He felt that they were such good people and he began to wonder if there was more than one way to God.

As time went on, he became more confident in the idea that there isn't one right way and certainly no wrong way to whatever God you believe in. As long as everyone is striving for the common human goals of peace, security, and love, then we all have something that connects us.

That's not at all how I grew up. My mom raised us in the Pentecostal Church, much to my dad's dismay. This faith showed that there is only one path to God. And that path included a lot of shame, rules on how you are supposed to dress, and loads of ritualistic crying and holy rolling.

Saeed's idea is a beautiful one, but I don't know how you make a belief system around it. Neither does Saeed, though. He keeps trying various things, hosting different events with the idea of bringing various people together. Today, in Sedona, he hosted World Peace Day. Sedona is the perfect place for something like that, what with all its energy vortexes where people claim to be healed of illnesses by meditating near them.

Kasim and I, of course, planned to leave work early and drive up there. Saeed and I left work at the same time. He headed straight to Sedona, and I went home to take care of Milani before heading out. I was starting to feel a little off anyway, so I was glad of the opportunity to leave work early. At first it just felt like typical morning sickness. Mine hasn't been too bad; I've been nauseated and living on mostly toast as everything else sounds terrible. Today after I came back in from taking Milani for her walk, a sharp, stabbing pain shot through my abdomen. It has never been this bad before, even in my worst moments of dealing with endometriosis. I fell to the floor, curled in the fetal position, crying from pain. Milani knew something was wrong. She came over to me, licked my face, and laid next to me, comforting me in that beautiful way that only an animal, in her pureness, can do. At one point, I was able to move just enough to reach the coffee table and grab my phone. I called Kasim.

"Kasim," I barely got out through heavy breathing and

crying, "Kasim, I'm hurting so bad. What if I'm losing the baby? Oh my God. I'm so scared."

"It's okay. I'm coming home now. Do you have the birth center's phone number? Didn't they give you one for emergencies?"

"Yeah, it's in that binder she gave me. Ugh, it's upstairs!"

I crawled up the stairs, Milani by my side every step of the way, and found the binder from Blossom. Just like Kasim said, there was an emergency number on the first page. I dialed it immediately.

"Hello, this is Angela."

"Angela, it's Suzanne." I told her my symptoms as best as I could between sobs. She gave me exact instructions and I hung up just as Kasim was coming in. Thank God his office is nearby.

He ran up the stairs two at a time and found me on the floor of our office loft, with Milani resting her head on my legs.

"Are you okay?" he asked, slightly out of breath.

"Yeah. It's lightened up a bit. But Angela said we should go to the hospital. She called St. Joe's to let them know we're on the way." He pulled me up off the floor and helped me downstairs.

In the car we made two phone calls—one to my mom, who met us at the hospital, and one to Saeed, to tell him we weren't going to Sedona tonight for World Peace Day. Saeed was worried about me and the baby, but he was already on his way to Sedona and there was nothing he could do; we insisted he go along with his evening as planned.

I began to feel better on the way to the hospital and I

wondered why. *Was it just some weird pregnancy pain that is new to me and is now gone or did I lose the baby and that process is over?* I stared out the window as I let this thought wash over me. What if she didn't make it? (Before I got pregnant, I decided I'm having a girl.) I'm ten weeks along, the first trimester is usually when a woman miscarries, so it isn't unreasonable to conclude this. *Am I okay with losing her?* I started to wonder about my maternal attachment to the baby. If I were a better mother, maybe I would just know if my baby was okay. Or maybe that's stupid and I just watch too many movies. And that's when it hit me; every major life event that occurs has been portrayed in movies and television in such a specific way that we think that's how life really is. I realized I was expecting to feel as a character would, that inside my head, there is an amalgamation of every character who has experienced something like this. I was feeling the emotions I'd remembered from movies and TV, and I realized that there really seems to be only one way to react to a moment like this if, indeed, I did lose the baby.

There's the expectation of grief and heartache. But would I be heartbroken and grieving? Or would I be talking myself into those things because of the narrative we are used to seeing? How do you grieve over something that you have yet to connect with? I don't know when a mother creates that connection. Perhaps it happens at conception and I am just not in tune enough, or sensitive enough, or maternal enough to create that bond, that beautiful bond people speak of between a baby and the woman who is her life source.

I shut down my thoughts. I knew I was going down a dangerous path or at the very least an unpleasant one. I closed my eyes and let myself drift off to sleep until we arrived.

I didn't lose the baby.

After what felt like forever, we (Kasim, my mother, and I) were taken out of the ER and to a different floor where I was to receive an ultrasound. The technician wouldn't allow anyone in the room with me, so Kasim and my mom waited in the hall.

I saw my little baby. And everything was fine. I saw a tiny little body and a giant, alien-like head, and it was the cutest thing I have ever seen. A sense of relief washed over me. There was my little creation, safe and sound, in her home. I don't know why, but I was slightly surprised by my relief. In this moment, I realized I was feeling my own emotions, not merely those I'd seen in movies and TV shows.

I don't know what's going on in Sedona for Saeed's Peace Day, but I felt a different kind of peace tonight, one where I know things will only get better. I had my one scare and now it's fine. We're all okay. I'll rest easy tonight.

SEPTEMBER 20, 2014:
THE CALL I DIDN'T MAKE

I have 1,001 cousins. One of them is named Natalie. She's been married for a few years now and so desperately wants a baby. They tried the natural route and it didn't work. So they've switched course and are trying IVF. They've done it two or three times now with no success. And ole Fertile Myrtle over here, I got pregnant on my first try. I'm sad for her. I needed to tell her that I'm pregnant before she heard it from anyone else. So tonight I decided to call her.

Before I did, I put myself in her shoes and imagined the phone call that would take place between us:

"Hey, Suz! What's up?!"

"Hey! Nothing. Just making dinner. How are you?"

"Good, just about to go to bed, everything okay?

"Yeah, everything is fine. I just...I, well, you see, the thing is...you'll be happy to know...uh, I'm pregnant."

Hold for the longest pause in the universe while Natalie, who must be unsure of how she feels about it, is trying to get herself together. At this point I know what she must be thinking:

God dammit. Was she even trying to get pregnant? How does

she expect me to feel about this when she knows how hard it has been on me? Fuck this.

I texted her instead.

This way, if she doesn't want to reply or if she wants to cry about it, she can react however she wants.

Natalie is possibly the most gracious person I know. And she responded with nothing but love. Yet that doesn't change how I feel about it all. Why me and not her?

Guilt is a powerful emotion. It can prevent you from living your life as best as you can. It can make you think you don't deserve happiness. It acts as a sort of self-flagellation, insisting that we not only have no right to be happy, but we should be in a constant state of un-happy.

I'm going to try really hard to not let this happen to me. I tend to carry the weight of the world on my shoulders, feeling everyone's pain so deeply and not understanding why I'm allowed to have so much when many have so little. In the past I have allowed this thought to paralyze me into inaction. But I'm going to be a mother now, and I don't want to pass on my survivor's guilt to my little one.

Is it possible to be too empathic? Most people call this a virtue and I think it is. I've always felt others so deeply, I've agonized over the pain of the innocent caught up in war and famine and disaster. But to what end? I cannot help those millions of people any more than I can help my cousin. So is the alternative then to ignore it? I don't think that's right either. I believe in helping others. I know it's right to try to bless others when given the chance. It's not in me to just go along with my life and just wish for world peace. Actions matter.

The Stoics believe that if there is something you can do to help another, then you must. But if you're upset about something happening on the other side of the world and you are powerless against it, then you should return to your duty of taking care of yourself, your family, and the community that you can help. Stressing about events outside of your control does nothing to help the victims and just robs you of your own serenity. (I'm paraphrasing enormously. The Stoics are deep.) I can't tell if that's a harsh view, a pragmatic view, a kind view...I'm still mulling it over.

The more I learn about life, the more I realize that I know nothing.

NOVEMBER 1, 2014:
MATERNAL INSTINCT IS BOLLOCKS

Today we went for our anatomy ultrasound, aka gender-finding-out ultrasound.

Technically, the reason for this particular ultrasound is to see what's going on with the baby's body in terms of development; checking for the correct amount of fingers and toes, head size growing properly, organs looking good, etc....and the gender identity should be secondary. However, this is not the case. Really, you're lying there on the oddly comfortable table/bed, with your partner holding your hand, waiting for the technician to wrap up the boring, yet incredibly important, anatomy exam so she can tell you that your suspicions are confirmed and that you are indeed having a girl.

I've been calling the baby "her." You always hear women say things like "I just know" or "I can feel it." Feel what? Know what? What is your body telling you that makes you able to interpret gender as if you now possess the skills of a Seer? I've always wanted to be one of these people, the ones who just "know." But I'm not.

I've been calling it a girl because if I ever thought of myself having a baby, I always pictured a girl. I guess that makes sense.

When thinking of future children, in many ways, you're just seeing yourself as a child, so it makes sense that you would reflect your own gender upon the imaginary baby.

"I'm telling you. It's a boy. I make boys. It's my Punjabi sperm," Kasim smugly said earlier today as we were getting ready for work. He's been saying this since the very beginning with so much surety that it's almost impressive how confident he is in something that he only has a 50 percent chance of getting right.

"It's a girl. I think," I said with much less certainty. I have never been certain about much. I've always changed my mind; I was never certain I knew all the facts on a topic to make such a bold claim as knowing for sure. I've been sure of so little in my life.

I was sure marrying Kasim was the right decision. That's probably the only action I ever took with complete certainty. Everything else I did was because I had to or it was a total crapshoot. I do feel strong in my convictions. But convictions and intuition are two very different things. You can have one without the other. I think.

There are things I just know. Things that are intuitive to me. I can tell you what's right and what's wrong, but I cannot tell you why. It's just instinct. I think my mom instilled a strong moral compass inside of me. Deep inside where words cannot reach. So deep that perhaps it isn't in my body at all. Perhaps it's in my soul, floating around the quantum universe.

But this guy, the guy I married, everything he says, he says with such authority. Perhaps it's just who he is and this is who I am. Perhaps it's a gender thing. Men seem to be more assertive than women in stating a position on a topic. It seems they are afforded the luxury of the rest of us just assuming they are right. And later, if more facts have been presented and they are forced to change their stance, they can swing into it so easily, whereas, for us, at least for me, new facts mean that I didn't take in all the information I could have, that I was too hasty. So over time, we quiet ourselves, shrink ourselves down a bit, to make room for the men that seem to know more.

And god dammit, the man was right. We're having a boy.

Instantly, every image I'd had in my head of a little girl with big curly hair and eyes as large as an owl's was replaced with a little baby Kasim. All of my thoughts were rearranged to accommodate a different reality. I don't know the first thing about raising a boy. I have one brother but he was surrounded by three sisters, so he usually deferred to our ways. Now I must raise a boy, help turn him into a man who will be respectful of women, treat them the way they should be treated. I don't take this task lightly. But where to start, I have no bloody idea.

NOVEMBER 17, 2014:
A MIRACLE

I feel I am beyond words, but I'll see what I can do. As I've mentioned, Natalie has been trying to have a baby for a while and I felt so guilty for getting pregnant so easily. Well, a couple of weeks ago, this happened…

"So, since we have so many viable embryos, they're gonna implant them in both me and Michelle, my surrogate, and that should double our chances that one of us gets pregnant. The doctors seem hopeful." Natalie was finishing telling me what the latest news was in her life regarding, as I like to call it, "The Great Matter."

"That's great! Okay, I don't want to get too excited, but I can't help it. When will we know if it worked?"

"We do the implantation tomorrow and then we have a blood test in two weeks. And we get the results the same day. So two weeks from now, if I call you, that means it worked. If you don't hear from me…" Natalie stopped abruptly. I know she doesn't want to think about that. She's had too many disappointments in this department and it's fatigued her.

I wanted to tell her that I know I'll get a call from her, because it will have worked. But I don't know that. False hope seems like a cruel thing here. I'm really bad at comforting people or saying the right thing. I prefer to be a good listener. So I didn't respond right away and gave her the space to take a couple of breaths and finish her thought in her mind. I didn't need her to say it out loud.

"Well, anyway, I should go. Hopefully I'll call you in two weeks," said Natalie.

"Inshallah," I said. Hoping for God's will seemed a useless thing to say but it was a good filler word.

Flash-forward two weeks later:

"So what's this audition for?" Kasim asked me as I was putting on my camera-ready makeup.

"It's a callback for that Clean Elections Campaign. Needing to make a commercial about the need for clean elections makes me sad at humanity," I said as I put too much contouring powder on my cheeks. "If a politician doesn't win honestly, that can't make them feel good. And what does that say about the state of American politics that this is something we have to contend with? We're better than this, aren't we?"

Kasim came around and kissed my cheek, forcing me to reapply the contour. "You think this because you're a good person. We're talking about politicians here. Politicians tend to be scum."

"Yeah, that's true," I said.

I drove to the audition with my makeup intact, my wavy hair behaving itself for once, and uncomfortable business attire constricting my legs. I was reciting my lines out loud in

51

the car when the phone rang. It was Natalie.

"Oh my God, Natalie! It's been two weeks. Tell me."

"I'm pregnant!" she said in an excited whisper—she must have still been at the doctor's office. I began to cry. I couldn't get any words out. All I could manage was happy squeaking noises. "Okay, I gotta go. I have to call more people. Bye." And she hung up. I looked in my rearview mirror. My makeup was ruined and for some reason I was shaking. Now I had to compose myself and run my lines one more time as I pulled into the parking lot. I didn't care. I didn't care if I got the role. Natalie was having a baby.

I went inside, did a terrible job, and thirty minutes later walked back to my car. I checked my phone and found another missed call from Natalie. Nervous, I immediately called back.

"Hello? Natalie? Is everything okay?"

"Michelle's pregnant, too," Natalie said through tears.

"WHAT?! TWO BABIES?!" I yelled as my tears were making a comeback. I couldn't believe it. She spent years trying to have just one, and now she is going to have two. At the same time. Twins, for all intents and purposes. Twins. I can't get over it. It's like I'm watching a real life Oprah story.

Privately, I wondered how hard it was going to be. She doesn't live anywhere near family. I imagine one baby is hard enough, but two...and can she ever be frustrated or annoyed? Or will it come off as ungrateful?

Natalie is about to get everything she's prayed for. But being a mother is hard. Can she ever express her hardship? One cannot live in a constant state of bliss. Regular, everyday life can't sustain in that state. I hope she isn't made to feel guilty for being stressed in all the same ways most mothers are stressed throughout the course of parenting. But for now, I know her heart is bursting with gratitude. For now, we all thank God and modern medicine for this miracle.

For now, we celebrate.

DECEMBER 20TH, 2014:
BABY SHOWERS ARE THE WORST

I will never think otherwise. They really are the worst—what with the "how quickly can you chug juice out of the baby bottle" game while your aunts horrify you by making dirty jokes about sucking and the "what kind of poop-looking candy is in this diaper" game. How old are we? Note to future self: Consider playing the poop game for my child's fifth birthday party.

As much as I hate them, my cousin Sommer did throw me a baby shower. It was very kind of her. I told her I didn't want a fuss but I have loads of relatives in town for Christmas so it made sense to celebrate the baby. I made a point to tell her that we shan't be playing any sort of ridiculous games so she kept it basic—a word search game and measuring the baby bump. It was tolerable.

It was a full house at my Uncle Hani's place, packed with uncles, aunts, cousins, distant relations from the mother town whose names I never really picked up on, and two friends. Yes, just two friends. Norah and Kristen are the only two girl friends that I invited on account of I don't have many girl friends in Phoenix. I have exactly two. The rest live elsewhere and I never bothered to make any more. It's mostly because most people annoy me. I always manage to find things that bug me about a person and then decide why even bother. I'm aware of this horrible flaw of mine. Alright, fine, I'm a judgmental ass. Happy?

But Norah and Kristen are cool. Norah, who I met working at Hollister when I first moved to Phoenix and needed a job, is the kindest person I've ever known. She has, as I like to say, one face. Most of us are two-faced, if not many faced, our faces changing as we go along in the world coming across different people and scenarios. But not Norah. She has one face. And it's a wonderful, kind face and I'm grateful to call her my friend. Kristen, an actor friend, is everything I'm not; she's blond with porcelain skin, speaks so eloquently, is giving, and feels emotions so deeply that she can cry at the drop of a hat. She's a damn angel.

The poor girls seemed so lost in the middle of this Arab fest, with my aunts yelling to people in Arabic, the men playing backgammon while drinking Turkish coffee, and the food looking, I'm sure, very exotic. But they kept their wits about them and sat among us as we fell into the rituals that accompany a baby shower. One of these rituals was the sacred unwrapping of the gifts as if I've been presented with frankincense from an ancient wise man.

Man, I'd kill for some frankincense. Instead, I received baby clothes, diapers, a stroller, a car seat (an incredibly thoughtful gift from the distant relatives whose names I can't remember), some sort of baby-don't-move contraption where you put the baby in a seat that holds them in place and they are encircled with toys all around them to stimulate them as they sit. It sort of looks like a baby office. Oh, and books! We got loads of books to start a little baby library for our boy. If that kid doesn't grow up to be a reader, I have failed as a parent. It's something I so desperately want him to love.

I digress.

The shower: all in all, it was every bit as uneventful as any other successful baby shower.

My favorite part of the day:

My cousin Nicholas and I grabbed the gifts that my loving family and friends bestowed upon me and my little guy and headed outside to put them in my car, our arms piled so high with gifts that we couldn't see over the top of them. As we approached my vehicle, Nicholas stuck his head to the side and said, "Of course. Of course you drive a Prius," and proceeded to laugh and roll his eyes.

I've always had a reputation on my mom's side of the family for being out of their ordinary. I say "their" ordinary because I'm probably perfectly ordinary to your average Joe. But these are not your average Joes. These are your average Khalids, if you will. My assimilation into American culture was more varied than theirs.

Some immigrants come here and find their own little versions of home: little Italy, Chinatown, etc. My relatives in Michigan live among the largest population of Arabs outside of the Middle East. Most of their friends are fellow Arabs, they get to continually speak the language and visit small businesses that sell knifah, pita bread, and the evil eye. Their church's congregation mostly consists of Arab Christians, trying to find a place of worship that is similar to what they knew back home.

In St. Louis, where I grew up, there weren't many of us Arabs. Our friends were White and Black, our church had very little diversity, and outside of our family, there wasn't anywhere else you could go for authentic food. So we assimilated into a more mainstream America that appeared so different from my cousins' America.

As kids, my cousins were always quick to make a comment about it; my chucks weren't something any of the Arab girls would ever be caught dead in, punk music wasn't music to them, and the fact that I didn't wear lip liner was abhorrent to them.

But we're family and we love each other. You find ways to laugh about your differences, to find common ground where you can. You argue about politics and then go on about the rest of your day together talking and laughing about other things because at the end of it all, you're family and there's no getting away from it. Family isn't black and white. It's not even gray. It's brown—muddy and messy, yet somehow beautiful.

I can't wait to introduce my kid to my culture. As a modern woman, there's loads about it that drives me crazy. But there are things that I love with my whole body. Most notably is our village songs, ancient chants that have been passed down from one generation to the next, not on paper, but through dance and celebration. Our little town of Bethlehem has never had much, but we have resilient spirits that know the importance of celebrating as many moments as we can and blessing each other through it all. We, in the new world, are trying to carry them along lest they be forgotten.

JANUARY 15TH, 2015:
A HOME TO CALL HOME

"It's $126 per square foot. That's the lowest price in our entire zip code. We're basically stealing the condo at this point. We'll never see anything like this. I think we should take it," Kasim said with his usual air of certainty. We have a small apartment that doesn't feel very child friendly, so we've been on the hunt to finally buy our own little place.

Bilbro, our realtor, who I try really hard not to call Bilbo, was showing us yet another condo. We had just driven away from our last one and Kasim was doing Kasim Math; that's when he maths so good and presents the numbers in such a way that you are left in awe. It's a wondrous skill that I can't wrap my mind around. Me, I don't math good.

The condo was empty. There was no staged furniture to show you the unrealistic way you could potentially not live. It was hard for me to picture it and it didn't stick out to me as anything special. But Kasim wouldn't shut up about how it's the best price we've seen considering the location. If we got it, we'd be within walking distance of a major intersection with loads of stores, a park, and, soon, my mother-in-law.

The baby is due in April. It's January now. It doesn't take

Kasim Math to work out that we need to make a decision soon. "I suppose the place is okay. It really is priced well. We'd be paying way less than we thought. Maybe we could take that extra money and put it into making the condo nicer," I told him later that night as we were brushing our teeth and wrapping up our discussion on the topic.

"I promise you, this is a good idea," he said as he took a shot of mouthwash.

"Okay. Okay, let's do it. Call Bilbro and have him put in an offer," I said with butterflies.

That was yesterday. Today they accepted our offer. And just like that, ladies and gentlemen, we're homeowners (pending an inspection and loan approval).

So this condo, priced at $126/square foot, is where our baby will spend the earliest part of his life. It will be where he says his first word, takes his first steps, eats his first solid food. (I don't know if I said any of that in chronological order. What happens first, I have no idea. Maybe I should read a parenting book.)

MARCH 5TH, 2015:
I WAS TORTURED TODAY

Kristen's kid, Chase, was turning four, and naturally we were obliged to go to his birthday party. The fact that it was at a train park was the cutest thing about the entire ordeal. The train park has an old world feel to it, with a general store, a carousel that plays old Disney songs, and, of course, a cute little train that you can ride all through the park.

Being there was like falling into a different time, a time where things were simpler. A time where you had a hard day working your land, but you made a point to finish early because the fair is in town and you promised the children you would take them and what's more, your husband promised you that he would look after them at the fair so you could wander around on your own and have a bit of a break from being both farm laborer and mother. So you do indeed wander on your own, while reluctantly keeping an eye on your family. After some time, you find a nice bench to sit on while you drink your cider and people-watch. You know you should probably be making the rounds, socializing with more acquaintances you keep seeing walk by in the distance, but you don't. The desire to sit alone, to be in your own thoughts, to quietly analyze other people and their behavior, is more thrilling than anything else and you'll be damned if anyone is going to tell you how to spend your child-free time.

Pregnancy Fact #2,838: When you begin to truly look pregnant (and not merely like you ate too many tacos) the other adult humans around you are incapable of talking to you about anything other than procreation.

We made our way through the masses of gazebos where countless children's birthday parties were taking place, finally finding the one we were invited to. We only knew a few people at this party as now most of our friends' friends consist of other parents, friends that they have had to make in order to maintain some semblance of a social life with a child in tow.

Our friends spotted us and we engaged in the customary "hellos" and received kind "congratulations!" and "oh my God, you're so big now!" We were forced to introduce ourselves to the friends of friends. These are parents, mind you. People who are currently in the trenches, and I swear to God you can see it on their faces.

Pregnant or not, this was my first experience in a social setting surrounded by parents and young children that I was not related to. I felt like an anthropologist dropped off in the middle of the Amazon, experiencing a way of life I have never seen before.

I was immediately accepted into this strange parental tribe, my stomach being a sort of homing beacon telling them that

I was not only permitted into this tribe, but was a temporary deity of the tribe, a goddess, creator of life.

At first, I rather enjoyed the attention. I'm an actor; we live for attention. But I started to notice, as Pregnancy Fact #2,838 clearly states, no one could talk to me about anything other than my pregnancy.

A slightly exaggerated compilation of many conversations formed into one for the sake of brevity:

"Hi, I'm Suz."

"Hi! I'm Erin [name changed to protect Erin's privacy and annoying character]. Oh my God, you're glowing! How far along are you?"

"Oh, thank you," I said in a tone of false modesty, absentmindedly rubbing my belly. "I'm eight months. So, how do you know the birthday boy?"

"Our children were in the same music class. They seemed so cute together so we decided to have a playdate and we've all been friends since."

At this point, I wasn't feeling too connected to Erin, so I attempted to move on. I wasn't so lucky.

"That's my boy over there in the conductor hat," she said, pointing to some kid next to a bunch of other kids.

"Aw, how sweet. He's cute."

"M-hm and he's sooo smart, oh my God. He's only four years old and he can already count to 500, if you can believe it! Boys seem to really enjoy numbers. Do you know what you're having?"

"Me? Oh. I'm having a baby." (Hold stare and pause for response.)

"Hahaha, oh my God, you're hilarious! Are you having a boy or a girl?"

"A boy."

And then comes my all-time favorite part. I'm not really judging here. We ALL do this. No matter the answer to the questions "What are you having?" or "How old is your baby?" or "What's your baby's name?" it is always, without fail, followed by the exact same response from every human being on the planet...

"Aaawww," Erin said to me excitedly. She was a Boy Mom and now I am too. I have moved from one of many deities in the tribe to standing before the queen of the goddesses, one who has gone before me and has taken an oath to pass on her wisdom to the next goddess that presents herself before the Fetal Temple.

"You're going to love having a boy," she continued, without my needing to chime in at all. "You'll probably be at the train park all the time. And oh my God, the dinosaurs and *PAW Patrol*, it's adorable."

"Wow. Uh, I don't know what that patrol thing is, but that sounds fun," I said, lying through my teeth. It did not sound fun at all. What the hell is a dog patrol? Her eyes were locked on me. I was the only person in her world and she absolutely had to train me in her Boy Mom ways. I had no desire to talk about my kid's potential love for dinosaurs and trains. I don't know this kid yet. Currently, my only thought is how much it's going to hurt when I push him out of me.

She wasn't going to let me go, so I attempted to switch topics. "So, are you from Phoenix?" This is always a good question as there are so many transplants in this city.

"No. We're from Colorado. We moved here before the baby was born to be closer to my husband's family. Is your family here to help with the baby?"

My God, she brought it back. How did she do that?

"Yeah, we have family on both sides. It's nice. So what do you and your husband do?"

"I'm home with my son. His name is Ryan, by the way. And Jeff is in real estate, which is great because that means his work schedule is pretty flexible so he can help me with Ryan if I ever need it. You're gonna need breaks whenever you can get them. Don't be a hero!"

There was no getting out of this. I gave in. I shut off the part of my brain that enjoys stimulating conversation and I let the autopilot small talk take over. At this point, more women were coming up to me and beginning this exact conversation again. Thankfully, Erin was a good listener and answered the other goddesses' questions on my behalf with as much enthusiasm as she most likely had when presenting Ryan to the tribe.

A very new, very strange sensation came over me. My insides felt heavy. I was no longer aware of the lovely breeze. My eyes couldn't stay focused. And the strangest sensation of all—I knew what it was like to have a dementor suck the joy out of your body[1]. I was experiencing it at that moment; my brain was searching for a reason to be happy, searching and searching. But the more it searched, the fewer memories it could conjure up. Anything good that had ever happened to me was slowly slipping and the only thought I had left was "this is my life now."

There's some crazy stuff happening in the world as I write. Palestine and Syria are under siege, the American elections are looming, and Congress is, well, they're the same as usual but that's a problem. Yet nothing real matters to these people. They have a sort of baby fever that has continued from pregnancy into parenthood. I was seeing my future, my very near future, and it did not involve intellectual or creative conversations.

I can't live like that. It'll break me.

We were the first people to leave the party. Kasim seemed to enjoy catching up with Kristen's husband. They used to be best friends, but haven't seen each other much since he became a dad four years ago. I felt bad making Kasim leave, but I had to get out of there. I couldn't be around those people any longer.

I came home and spent the rest of the day on the couch, with that heavy feeling never letting up. What am I going to do? I don't want to just be a mom. I'm more than that, aren't I?

I was seeing my new life being played out: mom jeans, play dates where we only talk about parenting, finding awkward

---

1 Dementor: a magical creature from the Wizarding World of Harry Potter that guards the wizard prison, Azkaban. Dementors don't kill you, but they can suck all happiness out of you until you have nothing left. Essentially, they kill your soul.

ways to get the kids to not fight with each other and just share the damn toy, desperately going out of my way to find mom friends because what single person is going to want to hang out with me as I chase a small person around trying and most likely failing to anticipate said child's needs? Oh my God, I'm going to end up driving a minivan. This all sounds horrible. But I'm eight months pregnant. I'm stuck with the decision I've made. I'm at the cusp of it all being very, very real and I've now realized that I might have made the wrong decision.

MARCH 25, 2015:
FAMILY MATTERS

"Come on! We're gonna be late!" I called out to Kasim as I walked back in the house after Milani's afternoon walk.

Fizza's family, her parents and two brothers, live in Pakistan. She hasn't seen them in five years. They have yet to meet her daughter. And today, they made their way to America, to live.

Fizza is an incredibly family-oriented person. She wants us there for every major family moment. When she was pregnant with Aliyah, she invited us to the ultrasound gender reveal. There we all were, packed into a tiny room to see the results live—Saeed, Kasim, Hassan, and I all standing, squashed into a corner as the technician told Fizza she was having a girl. Though we were indeed delighted, it was 7 a.m. We congratulated her and went straight back home. It was too early to be up and about, even for good news.

A couple of years later and here we are, another big family moment. A few weeks ago, Fizza dropped by to pick up meat pies that my mom made for Hassan. She knows they're his favorite.

"Would you come to the airport with us? I'd love for you to meet my family."

POSTPARDON ME

"Of course, Fizz. That sounds lovely. I'll even take my new camera and try to get some good shots of the reunion. Are you excited? Nervous? I mean, they're gonna be living with you guys—the four of them—in your tiny apartment."

Fizza thought about her answer as she pet Milani, who was snuggled up against her leg. Milani used to be Fizza's dog. Hassan got her a puppy when she first moved to America and didn't yet have a work visa. I didn't know Fizza very well at the time. When she moved here after marrying Hassan, I'd just started dating Kasim. We were not in a "wanna hang out with my family" kinda place. We were in a "let's spend all of our time alone at your place" kinda place. So Fizza spent all her time at home, lonely, while Hassan worked twelve-hour days. Milani was to be her companion. My, how things have changed. After Fizza gave birth to Aliyah, she could no longer stand the dog. She had no patience for the poor, attention-seeking puppy when all of her maternal instincts were focused on another tiny creature.

About a year after Aliyah was born, they went on a family trip to Seattle and Kasim and I took care of Milani for three weeks. Something clicked between the two of us. I'd never really cared for Milani before. She licked a lot and it drove me crazy. And just like people, I think there are some animals you connect with and some you don't. She and I were not soulmates. I won't get into the time she peed on me.

I'd never had a pet before. Pets are not a normal part of Arab households. My immigrant parents kept up this part of our culture, telling us that animals are dirty and do not belong inside. Whenever we played with the neighborhood dogs my mom yelled out, "Go wash your hands seven times! With soap!" So I never understood the bond between humans and their animal companions.

But then, just like a human relationship, Milani and I gave each other a second chance. She was forced to rely on me for her care. This, in turn, made me see her in a different light. She was this sweet, quiet dog who licked too much because she wanted so much love. I saw that desire in her for affection and it pulled at something in me. Perhaps it was some deeply hidden maternal instinct that I didn't know I had. In that time, with her human family away, she allowed me to love her.

When everyone came home from Seattle, I returned Milani to her home. Hassan said she moped around and didn't perk back up until I came to visit a week later.

Fizza, at this point, was struggling with balancing motherhood and work (not to mention her marriage and keeping up with household chores). Milani was just one more thing.

"Can I keep her?" I begged. "You don't have time, and she and I have bonded so much. Plus, being with me, you guys can still see her whenever you want."

"Take her," Fizza said without so much as a pause.

And one month later, I was pregnant. Figures.

So I watched Fizza stroke Milani as she thought of her answer to my question.

"Well, I have been used to being alone since I moved here. But in Pakistan I lived in a house with other family members, uncles and aunts and cousins, so I'm used to that too. I miss it sometimes."

"Well then. Good. I'm glad you're happy. I can't wait to meet them."

And now, finally, the day has come. I can't imagine how Fizza got anything productive done today. She must have been counting the minutes until we all headed out to the airport.

Kasim finally made his way downstairs. "Sorry. I had to change into jeans. Why did I decide to start wearing suits to work? They're so uncomfortable."

"Try being a woman—both jeans and suits are uncomfortable."

"And that's why I say you should only wear yoga pants. They're comfortable for you, sexy for me," he said with a wink.

"So that's our option, is it? Either we're really uncomfortable or we're wearing something that we all know is inviting men to stare at our asses," I said.

"You could always wear sweats," he said with a shrug.

"We haven't gotten that far yet. Maybe after the baby is born."

I grabbed my purse and my new Nikon and followed Kasim to the car. My stomach was in knots. There was this feeling of dread that hit me when I mentioned sweatpants after the baby. Lately, whenever I think of the baby coming and what my life will really look like, panic washes over me. I begin to wonder if

I've made the right decision in wanting to have a baby.

I think I've montaged it[2]. You see people with kids and the kids are adorable and the moms seem tired, of course, but they seem to love their kids so much that it's never even a question of if they got it wrong. But what if I did? What if everything I imagined is off the mark?

I've put together this reel in my head; Kasim bringing me chai in bed while I lovingly nurse the baby. Seeing him crawl for the first time. His first word and how proud of him I am at that moment. His knack for asking really hard questions about life. His desire to be a rebel with a cause. The way he looks like Kasim as he grows. How easy it is to travel with him all over the world because he's been doing it since he was born...

I've put all these images in my head and now I'm kicking myself. Of course it isn't going to be this way. Everything I'm reading now talks about nipple pain from nursing, needing to limit my caffeine intake, baby-proofing the house for when he starts to crawl, how multilingual babies tend to have delayed speech, and a child's need for structure and routine that make it sound like long-term travel wouldn't be ideal.

My body jolted. "Whoa!" I said, my hand going straight to

---

2 To montage: picturing something using a compilation of images in your mind that makes a situation look more picturesque, more movie-like, much like a montage from a film. Similar to Graduation Goggles* except this is looking forward rather than looking back.
* Graduation Goggles: a nostalgic feeling, looking back over a time you had with someone, remembering it fondly even though it was a miserable time. (See *How I Met Your Mother* S:6, E:20 for full details.)

my stomach. "That was the biggest kick I've felt!" Kasim put his hand on my belly in the hopes that the baby would kick again. When he did, Kasim smiled. But I knew better. It wasn't just a delightful kick as the baby swam around. It was a kick of fear— he knew my thoughts, he sensed my panic, he was calling out to me, reminding me of my duty as his mother.

My body got heavier and heavier as joy left me, replaced with dread for my child's arrival and guilt for feeling said dread.

And now I have to fake it at the airport as we watch a touching family reunion. I told myself I'm an actor and that this would just be a good moment to practice my craft.

Even in my sulking, it was undeniably beautiful. Fizza ran to the first person in her family that she saw walk past the security area and into the lobby. She let out a scream as she saw her big brother and ran to him faster than I've ever seen her run. She flung her arms around him and sobbed uncontrollably. And just when you thought that lump in your throat couldn't get worse, she hugged her mom. Her mother, looking exhausted, but with a smile glued to her face, embraced her only daughter and the two women cried. Soon it was everyone hugging everyone while I took photos and strangers stopped to watch this love fest unfold.

I wondered what the strangers were thinking, watching a bunch of Pakistanis reunite. I was hoping that it was a moment in which they saw the humanity in another group of people. I wanted them to think, "No matter where in the world you live or what you believe, family is family."

I'm about to start my own family. A husband and wife aren't considered a family apparently. It's not until that little addition comes along that you seem to officially be called a family. Family. It sounds so lovely to say. But the weight of having your very own that you are responsible for...I don't know if I can do it.

And in that moment, Braxton Hicks kicked in.

APRIL 11, 2015:
AND HERE WE GO

This might be the weirdest entry I'll make in my life. I'm in labor. Right now. But then why am I writing in my journal, you ask? Don't I have better things to do, you say? Not really.

This morning started out like a regular morning. Kasim and I slept in a bit then woke up and decided to make breakfast rather than go out as is our usual Saturday morning ritual. K was making a cup of coffee and as I was cutting Irish cheese to add to our meal, a trickle of warm water moved down my right leg. I don't know why, but I giggled. It felt funny and I was embarrassed. I thought I peed. Then there was another little trickle followed by more giggles. Now I know that I haven't peed.

"Did your water just break?" Kasim asked. "I don't think so," I said, thinking of all the movies and TV shows I ever saw. Water breaking usually was more of a huge gush of water, immediately followed by contractions. That didn't happen so that couldn't have been it.

"Call the birth center, just in case," Kasim said, pouring too much cream into his coffee while looking at me nervously.

He ran to get my phone. (I learned my lesson after the first time I needed to call my midwives in a hurry and I saved their number in my phone.) He called and put it on speaker.

"Hi, Angela," I said after hearing her slightly sterile greeting. "I have some water trickling down my leg. My due date is tomorrow. But it's not a rush of water or anything. And I feel fine."

"You're not in any pain? Any contractions?"

"No, nothing. I feel really good."

"Okay. Well, I'll tell you what, why don't you come on down and let's check you out and we'll go from there. You're right at your due date anyway. Can you come now?"

"Yeah. Of course. We'll be right there. See you soon."

Kasim hung up the phone and we looked at each other for a moment. Then we turned our heads, looking at our breakfast that was about to go to waste.

"I'll put the food in the fridge, you go get dressed," he said calmly, though the look in his eyes was anything but calm.

I threw on a light dress and we headed out the door. Thirty minutes later I found myself on that comfortable bed/table with my feet up in those uncomfortable holsters, while Angela did whatever she was doing down there. When her head reappeared she was holding a tiny bag filled with water.

"Yup, your water broke," she said, showing me the bag that she used to catch some of it.

"What does that mean?"

"It means that technically, you're in labor. But you're not having contractions yet, so you should just go home and rest. Your contractions should start soon."

Then she turned to the about-to-be dad. "Kasim, she's gonna need to rest up now. Make sure she eats a few light meals throughout the day. When her contractions kick in, warm showers are good, going for walks can help, but no baths." She turned back to me, "Once your contractions get so bad that you can't stand it anymore, call me and I'll have you come in. But try to stay home for as long as you can. You'll be more comfortable there. Call me with any questions. But for now, get some rest. Your baby is on the way!"

"Holy shit," I said a few minutes later as I was buckling up in the car. "I can't believe it's happening. We gotta tell the family."

I sent a message to my family chat that consists of just me, my parents, and my siblings. I then did the same thing for his side of the family. Immediately, Nancy called Kasim.

"Okay," he said after hanging up with his mother. "Mom is gonna make you your favorite pizza. I'm gonna take you home, then go pick it up. She's gonna prep it and we can put it in the oven whenever you're ready to eat. While you're lying down, do you mind if I lock myself in the office and send out emails? I'm gonna need to start delegating all of my work and wrapping up loose ends."

"Yeah, of course not. That's fine. I'm gonna watch *Friends*. Do what you gotta do," I said, rubbing my belly and sensing some anxiety kicking in.

And here I am. My contractions have arrived but as of now they're pretty far apart and the pain is manageable. I need to be distracted, so I thought I'd write. Who knows when I'll have time to write again.

I'm scared. I'm scared of how much this will hurt. I'm scared of life as a mother.

PART TWO

APRIL 30TH, 2015:
HE'S HERE

His name is Sammy. He was born thirty hours after my water broke. And I haven't slept since.

The birthing experience was fine.

Around 4 a.m. I couldn't bear it anymore. I called my midwife, it was Angela on duty tonight, and she told me to come on in. When we got there, I was greeted by a beautiful, warm bath. I labored in the tub as much as I could, letting the water relax my muscles and put me into a sort of trance.

My mom came a few hours later. That might have been the first time I stopped and really understood how much I needed my mom. Kasim was holding my body up during contractions and I rested on him in between, but my mom is my mom. She pulled my head onto her chest, cooled me down with a cold, wet cloth, and fed me by hand so I could have strength to get through labor. I never needed her more. She never had a natural birth and she was scared out of her mind watching her daughter wail, grunt, and experience pain no parent wants their child to go through. But the more I hurt, the stronger she became. I suppose that really is what it means to be a parent.

Soon, I was dilated at 10 cm. and it was time to push. Angela kept saying, "Bear down." I didn't know what that meant. I had never heard that phrase in my life. I felt stupid that I didn't know how to push. I'd always heard of these crazy birth stories where mothers would say that they just felt the need to push and next thing you know they've pushed out a baby in the car while their husbands are driving the minivan down the highway on the way to the hospital. I didn't feel that. I didn't know when to push. Angela had to tell me. I never thought I was going to be the most maternal mother, with instincts that rival Mary Poppins, but I just assumed that biologically, my body would take over and know what to do. The fact that it didn't frustrated me. I gave in to my midwife and let her expert hand guide me.

I was beyond fatigued. I had never experienced such exhaustion in my life. I wanted to give birth in the tub but it wasn't working. The water seemed to be pushing the baby back in. I lay on the bed and began the back-to-back series of pushes, then finally pushed my last push while Kasim held one leg and my mom held the other. And then it was over. Sammy was born. He was immediately thrust onto my naked chest so I could begin taking care of him.

I was all tears, barely able to see my child as the tears were steaming up my glasses. It was done. He was here. My emotions were indescribable. I couldn't, even now, tell you if I was happy or sad or relieved or what. I felt everything and nothing in particular. A few minutes later, I handed little Sammy over to Kasim so I could push out the placenta. (We never talk about this part. I find it to be completely fascinating. The life force that kept this child growing healthy and strong, the thing that connected us, that sent every bit of my energy to him, was now coming out of me. It was a strange experience, pushing a soft, pliable organ out of my body.)

As I watched Kasim hold Sammy, I was incredibly moved. Kasim cried more than Sammy did. He held him, bare chest to bare chest, working to create the physical bond as he openly wept. He didn't just experience a surge of hormones swirling around in his body as I did. His weeping was an expression of love. And I have to admit, it was the most beautiful thing.

Several hours later, with more energy than I thought possible after spending an entire thirty hours in labor, we took Sammy home. Naturally, I sat in the backseat, keeping an eye on Sammy while Kasim cursed every single person on the road. Clearly, they were all our enemy and actively trying to kill us. As I sat back there, I wondered why our midwife let us leave. She just handed over this tiny person and told us to look after him. Was she insane? How irresponsible could she be, giving him to two people who had never done this before?

I decided co-sleeping was what I wanted to do. Kasim didn't trust himself to sleep so close to something so squishable, so he slept next to us on the floor for two weeks. But, as I said, we didn't sleep. Every time Sammy made a noise we Googled it. "Hey Google, why does my newborn seem to have mini spasms all the time?" "Hey Google, what's this red dust in my newborn's diaper?" "Hey Google, what exactly is Sudden Infant Death Syndrome?" "Hey Google, did I just make a huge mistake becoming a mom?" (Google didn't answer the last one.)

I was suddenly so angry. We spent so much time taking a birth class learning how to push the baby out. No one told us what to do when we got home. No one mentioned that the red dust in his diaper is no big deal, for instance. How did people do it before Google, I wonder?

The next morning I attempted to get out of bed. I say "attempted" because it wasn't at all easy. My body ached, of course. But my entire body ached, even down to my bones. I couldn't walk. *Why am I so frail?* My body had had the shock of its life and didn't seem to know how to deal with it. For weeks this pain stayed with me. Every time I got out of bed, my feet hurt and I could barely step down on the floor. My arms hurt to the point where it was difficult to even pick Sammy up. I did pick him up, of course. What else was I supposed to do?

We decided early on that we didn't want everyone visiting us at the birth center after Sammy was born, just like our midwife suggested. I made this decision early on because I saw what Fizza went through in the hospital when she had her baby. It was terrible. She was shaking from the meds given to her for her C-section. She barely had the strength to hold her baby and there was an entire clan of people there to greet her and our newest family member. So when we were having Sammy, we decided that the family could come to the house the next day. I would be in the comfort of my own bed, there was more room for people to walk around and not crowd me, and most importantly, they would come on my timeline rather than pacing the waiting area handing out cigars and waiting to lovingly push in and see their new love that I'd just pushed out.

Naturally, everyone was over the next day—Kasim's mother, father, and brother, my three siblings, one cousin, and two parents (thankfully not all at the same time). At one point, toward the late afternoon, Kasim noticed that his mother wasn't holding Sammy as well as she should, taking care of his tiny neck. She is sight limited, blind in one eye and impaired in the other, so some things are a bit more difficult for her. Kasim said something to her about the way she was holding the baby and it hurt her feelings. A bit later, it was time to take her home. Kasim drove her home, three minutes away, but was gone for about an hour as he tried to assure her that he did indeed trust her with his baby, that he's just a paranoid new dad. I was left with my sister and cousin. They were about to go but I begged them to stay. I would have been left alone with Sammy. I couldn't have that. What if something were to happen? I have no idea what, but what if it did? I was petrified of being alone with my baby.

That worry hasn't gone away yet—the fear of being alone with him. Since then, I have, of course, been alone with him, but I don't like it.

And so that's that. He's here now. And it's my job to take care of him. From now on, all my thoughts are to be about the baby. I am to anticipate and understand his needs like some sort of wizard. I didn't even have the instinct to push. How do I find the instinct to take care of him? And what if I don't want to take care of him? He hurts me. Every time he wants to eat I cry. My nipples are raw and I don't want to feed him. I don't want him on my breast again. He'll be up soon. I can feel the milk filling up like a car tank filling up with gas. And I'm not ready. I'm not ready for him to hurt me.

You know the weird part? I tell him I love him. I say the words that I know I'm supposed to say. But I make myself say it. I am in no way compelled by my own soul to say loving things to him. What does that say about me?

MAY 7, 2015:
I DIDN'T DREAM IT

In *The Matrix*, Neo is offered the blue pill or the red pill: the blue one will provide him with a blissful life where he won't know a thing about what's actually happening, while the red pill will show him what life is really like, the truth, the bondage we are in.

I took the red pill on the day I gave birth. People say being a parent is hard. But that's such a generic statement. You are not just embarking on a hard path. You are embarking on a path that has nothing to do with you, yet you are forced down it, expected to mend the holes with very little instruction while looking out for wild animals that want to hurt your baby—and you have to kill them with your bare hands if need be. Yet you have never been in the wild before, you have an instinct hidden somewhere that makes an appearance now and then, a sudden, biological knowledge of exactly how to kill the bear that wants to attack your child. It's a quiet instinct, you can barely hear it, and it's muddled with other voices in your head telling you that you're tired, that the bear is too big, that you've never even seen a bear, that you are too scared, you are not capable of killing it, you are not capable of doing what needs to be done.

Sometimes when I'm alone with Sammy and he's crying uncontrollably, I start to lose my mind. I start begging, pleading with a God that I'm not even sure I believe in. "Please, God, don't let this be real. I don't want this. This was a mistake. Please let this be a dream. Wake me up!"

I honestly think this has all been a dream. It's as if I can see reality around me, but I'm in this bubble where I cannot access the real world. I'm only watching through a blur, barely able to concentrate from pure exhaustion. My body still hurts so much, I have a hard time thinking straight. Everything seems muddled, just like my dreams. I'm having a hard time understanding that this is my reality. I'm half convinced it isn't.

I can't even look at him. I can't look at Sammy. He's cute. He's bloody adorable, with his big gray eyes that are obviously going to turn brown and his jet black hair and his tiny little toes. But he's taking everything from me. He's depleting my body of sustenance. He's taken away my freedom. I'm stuck. And as much as I plead with God, I still haven't woken up. It's not a dream.

MAY 12, 2015:
DRUNK IN LOVE

I'm just kidding. I'm not drunk in love. I'm just drunk. Well, not drunk on alcohol. I'm so damn delirious that I've wondered if I drank and didn't know it. Most of the day it's a bit of a fog. I don't know how I manage to keep both Sammy and myself alive. Someone, give me a medal for doing so.

Sammy laughed today. Like, he really laughed. It was such a beautiful sound. I've heard people say that their favorite thing is their child's laughter. I get it. It's intoxicating. There really is nothing like it.

MAY 15, 2015:
YOU DRANK THE ONLY GOOD
THING GOING ON IN MY LIFE

It was a good day. It was actually a really good day. My mother-in-law came over in the morning and watched Sammy while I napped and showered. I did both! I didn't have to choose between napping or showering. What a luxury! Honestly, not having to take Sammy into the bathroom with me while I shower is a huge win. He seems to really like his Nana. He was so content that he didn't seem to need me. When can this woman move in?

But of course, nothing good lasts too long. By the afternoon, Sammy was back to his moody self and clinging to me. Are all children like this with their mothers? Do they scream if they are not near us? I would like to say that's a really beautiful thing, but how does one get anything done or recharge if one never gets time away from this leech, uh, I mean child? Any happy feelings that I stored up from my nap and shower were depleted halfway through the day.

"Would you like me to pick up some food for dinner, my child?" my father-in-law asked later that day while he was sitting on the couch. He came to visit Sammy but gave up any attempts at holding him. Every time I handed Sammy to him he screamed so loud there was just no point. (Sammy screamed. Not Saeed. I shouldn't have to explain this, but I'm tired and I don't know if anything I'm saying makes sense anymore.)

"Yes! I'd love that."

"You name it. Whatever you like, I'll go get it."

"I'd really love True Food. Is that okay?" I asked.

"Of course, my child. Just order it and I'll go get it."

I got online and ordered food for us all. I ordered my favorite drink from there—a Cucumber Refresher. I couldn't wait to drink it. I began to obsessively think about this drink. It was gonna fix everything. It was going to make me happy. I can't tell you why I had this revelation about this Happy Drink. It was a simple indulgence. Something yummy that had nothing to do with Sammy. It was a treat for me and no one else.

Later, Saeed walked in with brown paper bags filled with delicious smells.

"Thank you so much, Ami," I said, grabbing the bags from him as he made his way into the house. "No problem, my child," said Saeed.

"Food's here?" Kasim asked as he walked out of his home office. Saeed and Kasim sat in the living room while I took the bags over to the kitchen to begin dividing up the food.

"Yes," said Saeed. "You know, that's a wonderful restaurant," he continued. "What magnificent customer service. While I sat at the bar waiting for them to finish up the food, they offered me this delicious cucumber water. They didn't have to do that. That was classy."

Meanwhile, I grabbed plates and silverware and made my way to the bags of food. I looked for my Cucumber Refresher first. I couldn't wait until I was eating my dinner to start drinking it. I wanted it now. I couldn't find it. I started pulling things out of the bags for a better look. But it wasn't there. I frantically looked over the bags again, I looked behind the bags, I looked in the living room where they were sitting, I looked at the bench in the entryway. Nothing. No Cucumber Refresher.

I froze.

"Ami, did you say they gave you cucumber water while you waited for your food?" I asked with my fists in balls.

"Yes. Such excellent service," Saeed said with a twirl of his hand.

Tears began streaming down my face. I walked back into the kitchen unable to stop the flow of tears. I've been crying a lot lately. Crying is an incredibly uncomfortable thing for me. We don't cry in our family. And if I have to do it all the time now, I'd rather not do it in front of people.

"What's wrong?" Kasim said, following me into the kitchen.

"That wasn't cucumber-infused water that Saeed drank. That was the drink I ordered. The Cucumber Refresher. He drank it."

Kasim laughed. He freaking laughed. Then he made his way over to Saeed.

"You're an idiot, Pops. That wasn't excellent customer

service," Kasim said, still chuckling. "Suzee ordered that drink for her. You drank her beverage."

Now Saeed laughed. Why is this funny? "You paid for that? It just tasted like flavored water. What a silly thing to pay for."

And the bastards continued laughing.

You know that scene in *Friends* where Ross's boss ate the turkey sandwich Monica made him after Thanksgiving?

"That was the only good thing going on in my life. He ate the only good thing going on in my life!" Ross shouted in the coffee shop.

That was me today. Saeed drank the only good thing going on in my life. Then he was cruel enough to laugh about it. I couldn't eat. I took Sammy and went into my room and closed the door. It was almost Sammy's bedtime. I'm writing this now while I nurse Sammy. (I'm getting pretty good at multitasking.)

I've never been upset over a drink before. It's silly, I know. But I've also never been this unhappy before. I thought I was going to have a few moments of happiness. A drink to make me happy, to feel refreshed, as the name of the drink so aptly states. It was just one more disappointment. One more person who doesn't understand me or my needs or what I'm going through.

He's finally asleep. Time to close my eyes and not think about Saeed's betrayal.

MAY 23RD, 2015:
SHOULDA, COULDA, WOULDA

Sammy is a terrible sleeper. His sleeping patterns are all over the place. This kid will fall asleep while I'm feeding him, so I have to wake him up and start again. Sometimes it takes me an hour and a half to feed him. So I've started doing this middle of the night routine; when he starts to cry and it's time to eat, before grabbing him, I sit up, grab my iPad from my nightstand, and prop it up in front of me, then I grab Sammy out of the bassinet. (I finally put him in a bassinet so Kasim can have his side of the bed back.) We settle in and I watch *3rd Rock from the Sun* while Sammy nurses. Kasim can sleep through anything, so it doesn't bother him at all.

Watching that show is cathartic as I wait for Sammy to finish bloody eating so we can all go back to sleep. It's engaging enough to distract me from my reality, but not serious enough that I have to really concentrate. Sometimes while I'm watching it, my mind wanders. I imagine what it would be like to be on a show like that, entertaining millions of people, gaining fame as a comedian, being loved by the masses. I don't think I wanted to ever be a comedic actor, but now I'll never know, will I? Sammy took that away from me. He took away everything.

Here it is. I'm going to admit something that I can't say out loud. I don't like Sammy.

Last week:

It was a gorgeous day. Nature seemed to be giving us a bit of a reprieve from the steady, incremental heat that is on its way: a Phoenician Summer.

Naturally, I had family visiting. When your parents come from a small town in the Middle East, you are inevitably related to the entire aforementioned town; ergo, there is always family visiting. On this particular day, my Uncle Gabe, Aunt Krystal, and their son Nicholas were visiting. Kasim and I were sitting outside at Sommer's house, with our feet in the pool, talking to Nicholas, who was enjoying swimming in the warm weather while his home in Detroit still has the heat on. I was holding Sammy while I let his little feet splash about in the water. He seemed to be enjoying this new sensation. I really do enjoy watching him experience new things.

So things seemed really lovely at the moment. Nicholas was looking at his newest cousin and smiling.

"Who do you love more, Sammy or Kasim?" Nicholas asked in this odd Sophie's Choice sort of way. Without a single moment of hesitation or even thought, "Kasim," I blurted out. Nicholas looked at me with his mouth open. "Really?" he said after regaining a bit of composure. "Man, I don't know. I love my brother, but when his kids were born, I would gladly kill him to protect those kids. I'm crazy about them, dude."

I began to tense up. "But I know Kasim. I've spent years

cultivating a relationship with him. I don't know Sammy. All he does is eat and sleep." Clearly his initial query was strictly rhetorical.

"Oh my God, I like totally love Sammy more than Kasim. Like how is that even a question?" is what I should have said. Why is it that I have to instantly adore this tiny person over everyone else? Does everyone think the way Nicholas does? Is there something wrong with me? Maybe I'm broken.

Back to today:

So, I'm not crazy about my kid. But you're not allowed to say that to people. As evidenced by Nicholas, there is definitely only one way you are supposed to feel—yes, mothers are like goddesses, but goddesses were fierce and pissy and emotional. It's not easy goddessing.

I'm frustrated beyond words. It seems to me that I am this way for two reasons:

He's exhausting me. I can barely think straight. I'm just trying to make it through the day. I don't have time to think about how much I love this creature.

I'm starting to realize that his arrival means that I have squandered my child-free days. If I had been more aggressive, more intentional with my time, maybe I would be in a different place. I could have had a proper career. Maybe I could have made it as an actor. And now there is no chance for success in my life since I have been forced to toss aside my ambition. They say youth is wasted on the young. I get that now. To think of what I should have done, what I could have done, had I realized that having a kid would be my biggest obstacle against doing whatever it was I should and could have done. Where would I be right now? Sometimes it's as if I'm grieving for a life I never had. Sometimes I'm grieving for the beautiful life I used to have. And other times, I'm grieving for the future—the dismal, shitty future.

MAY 31, 2015:
SURVIVOR'S GUILT

I'm all over the place. Confused. I'm dealing with some familiar feelings but in a new way: Shame and Guilt.

Let's begin with shame, shall we?

Ah, shame. A concept I know so well. It's a feeling every Arab woman (probably most women, really) is familiar with. Good Arab girls are essentially supposed to sit around at home, acting like nuns until all the not-so-good Arab boys are done partying and sleeping around and are ready to settle down. Then we can be there to marry them. But God forbid if we had any fun of our own before we knew them. Any sexual feelings are shameful. Going out late is shameful. Hanging out with boys that aren't your brother or cousins is shameful. It's exhausting.

Then there's the Christian shame. The shame of sinning and disappointing God. Even thinking shameful thoughts is shameful. Wearing a skirt above the knee, showing your shoulders, wearing makeup—shame, shame, shame.

There are really beautiful things about both my Arab and Christian upbringing, but the constant shame is not one I look on fondly. I resent it very much. I've shed all of that as I entered adulthood. But just like an annoying song that makes its way into your head and you can't shake it, shame has made a comeback.

Shame has crept up on me as I realize how unprepared I am for motherhood. I don't know what I'm doing. I'm not at all confident about how to take care of Sammy. I thought so much of this was predicated upon instinct. How else have mothers done it since the beginning of time if not on instinct? Yet I don't seem to have it. I didn't even have the biological wherewithal to push out my own baby without being told.

I've had a lot of time to think; before I had Sammy I was starting to regret my decision to have a baby. Now I know I was right. This was a bad idea. I shouldn't have done it. And now I'm ashamed of my regret. What kind of person feels this way? Only a bad one, that's who.

So there it is: I'm ashamed that I don't know what I'm doing and even more ashamed that I don't love my baby the way I'm supposed to. And now all this shame is making me feel guilty. My God, how many feelings can one person experience? This is getting to be ridiculous.

Shame and guilt go hand in hand. When you're a teenager who has kissed a boy and you've been told it's shameful, you feel guilty.

When you secretly trimmed your hair even though it goes against the teachings of the church, that shame makes you feel guilty. They are two peas in a pod, best friends. Like good and evil, you cannot have one without the other.

My biggest guilt point is Sammy. He didn't ask to be born.

He didn't force himself into my world. And here I am imposing all of this negative emotion on him. This is only just occurring to me now, but is Sammy crying so much because he can sense my anguish? It would make sense. We've been linked, physically and emotionally, since his conception. And now the one person he trusts and needs the most is more than out of sorts.

It's weird to think about how much I dislike my own child when I spent so much time fighting for the rights and survival of other children. I used to fall asleep crying over the children of Darfur, desperately wanting to hold them and save them. I wanted to dedicate my social justice career to making sure that children, the most vulnerable of our human population, were taken care of.

When I was in college, I discovered the world of Human Rights. It was my major, my life. I learned about genocide in Sudan, child soldiers, environmental rights. I was completely immersed in it, watching documentaries and reading everything I could get my hands on. At one point, I starred in a play, as a journalist who goes to Sudan and sees the genocide up close. While working on the play, I was writing a brief for a law class on the same topic and spending my free time with the Amnesty International club talking about it. At night, when I closed my eyes, I would see the most terrible sights and hear the most terrible sounds. I ached. My insides were in turmoil. I could feel the pain and fear of those women running with their children on their backs. Who cared about a stupid play when people were dying? What good would it do? I began to cultivate a sort of survivor's guilt. I felt guilty for enjoying a warm shower, for getting into a proper bed, for having my pick of ridiculously overpriced coffee at the most famous coffee company in the universe.

I was seeing a new level of suffering, and I couldn't take it. It wasn't fair that I had so much when others had so little.

And yet.

Yet here is this one little boy who needs me and I'm angry he's even here.

Then, of course, there's the guilt of having it all and not being happy about it. Between my international human rights studies and work and spending time in my parents' motherland, I have come to be so grateful for the life I live. I want for nothing.

So when these weird bouts of sadness kick in, I can hear myself saying things like: *Oh, shut up. You're fine. You live in Phoenix, surrounded by resorts and world famous golf courses, you don't have to work, you get to stay home and take care of your healthy baby in your nice, safe condo. Shut the hell up.*

Guilt allows me to acknowledge the good things in my life. I'm still trying to figure out how to turn that guilt into gratitude.

I've never been so conflicted in my life.

JUNE 1, 2015:
THE ONE I GAVE UP

I read this book series a while back called *Ender's Game*. I really enjoyed it. I'd say the books are close to the top of my list of favorites. In the second book, humans have colonized about a hundred different worlds. Some had intelligent life on them already, some did not.

Ender happens to find himself on this planet called Lusitania. The humans are living among a native species that they call Piggies because they look like small pigs, but they walk on their back two legs. When the author was describing the Piggies, he described them exactly how you would describe a dog to an alien who has never seen one. They were smart, had their own language and practices. Even though they didn't have the same facial features as humans, they had similar emotions as humans but expressed them in different ways. It made me think of dogs, how they can be excited, but to us, their face doesn't really change that much, but we know they're excited by other ways they move their bodies.

I don't know why, but this was my "aha" moment. This was when I realized how wonderful, how beautiful dogs are. It suddenly occurred to me that just because I don't understand them doesn't mean that they are void of real emotion. I remember reading this part and being blown away by this realization. I don't know if the author intended for this comparison to be made, but that is what I got out of it. And what a beautiful thing.

I had never experienced this type of connection with someone that wasn't human. Bonding with Milani was so special.

Then I couldn't do it anymore.

Yesterday, late afternoon, Sammy, Milani, and I were driving in my little Prius, on the way to a park a bit farther away than our usual one. I fancied a change. As we were driving down a main road, my two little creatures in the back seat, Milani noticed a police car, lights flashing, on the side of the road. She ran to the other side of the car to get a good look, jumping on top of Sammy's body to gain height to see properly out the window.

"Milani! Get down!" I yelled, reaching one hand back there, attempting to grab her by the collar, while keeping the other hand on the wheel and my eyes on the road. She was too far away from me. "Milani!" Her tail wagged as she enjoyed the view and ignored me. Sammy started to cry. She was hurting him. I was frantic. Hysterical. But I couldn't pull over quickly. We were in the middle lane of a three-lane road during rush hour. I kept screaming her name over and over, scratching my throat, crying. As I kept screaming at her and attempting to pull her away with my right arm, I moved into the right hand lane so I could take the next right and pull over into an office complex. I didn't look for a parking spot. I swerved into the entrance, quickly making another right to be out of the way of oncoming cars, and jumped out of the car. I ran to Sammy's side of the car and pulled the car door open. Milani knew that I was angry and had moved away from Sammy by the time I made my way to them. I gently took my two-month-old out of his car seat, assessing him for bruises or cuts, checking his breathing. She had marked him. His legs had scratches on them from her hind legs pushing their way up. I held him while we both cried.

After we were both a bit calmer, I put him back in his car seat and sent Milani to the front seat so I could hold her collar and keep her away from my son. I grabbed my phone.

"Fizza," I said, attempting to stay calm. "You have to take Milani back. I can't keep her." I told her what happened. She was very understanding and told me that I could send her back but that no one was at her home right now. "Okay. I'm gonna send her to Nancy's house. She'll be waiting for you there."

After I hung up with Fizza, I called my mother-in-law, no longer able to keep back the tears, and told her what happened. "Aw, honey," she said sweetly. "Of course. You can bring her here. She can play with Zoey until Fizza comes to get her. Zoey would love having another dog to play with."

Does this make me a bad person? To claim that I love this

creature, to say that I've bonded with her, but so easily give her up? She hurt my baby. I can't think straight. The house is already weird without her. But I can't do it. I can't keep her. She had to go.

JUNE 4, 2015:
"KEEP YOUR FACE TO THE SUN AND YOU WILL NEVER SEE THE SHADOWS." – HELEN KELLER

I've noticed a pattern. Something weird.

I was warned of this strange phenomenon by a fellow new mom at the birth center, another woman in the trenches. I didn't think magic existed. And now I'm forced to contend with the darkest of magic. I have not taken enough Defense Against the Dark Arts classes to be ready for this.

Witching Hour.

At approximately the same time every evening, as the sun is setting and dusk's light has made its way into my home, confusing me with its inability to tell me whether or not it is day or night, something happens to Sammy. Just like a werewolf at the full moon, dusk brings a chaotic spirit into my child. He is inconsolable. Nothing makes him happy—eating, playing, bathing, resting...nothing. He will spend the next two hours angry.

It has started to seep into my psyche. When I'm not even thinking about it, but my internal clock knows dusk will soon be upon us, a sense of dread will begin to make itself known in my stomach. I will feel sick, nauseated. I will start to tell Kasim something is wrong. One day in particular, I walked into his home office. I needed help.

"What's wrong?" he asked, mid-email.

"I don't know," I said, placing my hand over my stomach the way you do when you think you are about to throw up. "I just know something is wrong. It's too dark in our condo. I really hate it. Can you take the screens off the sliding doors?"

Our condo really only gets light from one side of the house, through the front door, which I keep open all day. A large, glass security door allows me to bring as much light in as I can. In our living room are two large sliding glass doors leading to two different balconies, perpendicular to each other. Most Phoenicians would love that these two sides of our homes are flanked by trees, keeping our home cooler than normal. Not me. The trees block the sun coming in during the late afternoon, during the scariest time of my day. Any small thing I can do to let in more light, I have to do.

"You want me to take the screens off?" Kasim asked, confused.

"Yeah. It's too hot to open the patio doors anyway, so it's not like we need them. I feel better with more sunlight. Please."

"Okay, sure. But what's wrong with the light that's already in the house?"

"It's just not enough. I'm panicking. I'm freaking out. I know it sounds weird, but natural light makes me feel a

bit better. Please, can you just do it? Right now? Please."
I exhaled, exhausted, as if I had just given a speech at the
United Nations. Kasim and I looked at each other for a
moment, locking eyes. He was trying to understand this
person in front of him. He was looking for signs of his wife.
But she's not here right now. Neither one of us knows where
his wife went. He nodded, got up, and went straight to one of
the patios and started removing the screen door. I followed
him into the living room and glanced over at Sammy, who
was rocking back and forth in a swing. I knew what was about
to happen. I was nervous. I needed Kasim to move faster.
Light was the only solution I seemed to have to a problem I
didn't understand. He removed the first screen and a beam
of light fell across the room and onto my body. I soaked it in,
closing my eyes and letting it wash over me, cleansing me of
my pain. Then the next screen, more light, more cleansing,
less pain.

After experiencing this for several weeks, I have finally seen
the pattern and my comrade's words, the words of that fellow
mother, are coming back into my mind.

Witching Hour.

I now know it to be true. And the worst part of it is, there
is no defense against this daily curse. Much like the werewolf
attempts to function around the lunar calendar, biding his
time, I, too, wait for the time I cannot control.

Most days, Kasim isn't home at this time of day and I have
to do it alone. But he was here this time. He arranged the

screen doors outside, propping them up on a wall, and headed back into his home office. It was strange that he was working from home at all. I know he prefers to be at his actual office with his "supercomputer," as he likes to call it. It looks like a NASA control center, with two keyboards and five monitors. But about once a week, I've noticed he's working from home. I haven't said this out loud, but I think he's keeping an eye on me. You know, for a man, he's quite intuitive.

A few moments later, Witching Hour began. Sammy introduced the hour ("hour" being just an expression as it lasts anywhere from two to four) by suddenly screaming out of the blue. I walked over to the swing and picked him up. I comfort-nursed him. I knew it wasn't time to eat yet, but this is the happiest place for him and I'm always desperate at this time of day. After a few minutes, I settled us on the floor with a few toys and some books and attempted to entertain him. I picked a spot on the floor where one of the new rays of sunshine was making its way through. If I had to put a number on it, the extra light in our home decreased my panic by about 3.245 percent. It wasn't much, but I would take it. I would take anything.

It's not too strange to think that light might ease panic. Panic, anxiety, dread, is a fear of the unknown; is Sammy going to freak out? Am I going to know what to do? Is my night going to be horrific? Is that tension in the bowels of my stomach going to go away?

Light seems to push its way in, providing a bit of clarity,

showing you that things aren't as terrible as they seem in the dark. That the shadow on the wall is nothing. That monsters do not exist. That you will be okay. The sun will always be there for you.

JUNE 5TH, 2015:
I DON'T FEEL IT

I don't think I feel the thing. The thing you're supposed to feel when you look at your baby. I watch other mothers. I listen to other mothers. I analyze their words. Everyone seems to look at their children like they're the greatest thing they've ever set eyes on. I think Sammy is really cute, what with his jet-black hair, perfect light-brown skin, and those gray eyes. But most of the time when I look at him, I don't feel anything.

What is it that I'm supposed to be feeling? I'm half convinced everyone is lying. That they only say that because they think they have to. Because we've romanticized parenthood.

Or is it me? Is there something wrong with me? I'm not the most lovey-dovey person in the world, but you'd figure if I felt anything for anyone, it would be my own child. Sometimes I look at him, waiting to feel the thing. I try to talk myself into it. I tell myself how cute he is, how I love him, how he's my whole world. But I got nothin'.

I'm confused. I'm frustrated with myself. I'm annoyed at other women who either have something I don't or are lying about the entire thing. If it's the former, then I don't know what to do about it. If it's the latter, then that's a really cruel thing to do. Why doesn't anyone talk about how much this sucks? Or maybe for them it sucks, but they still feel the thing? I don't know! And I don't know how to get answers because I don't think anyone would ever admit to feeling the way I do.

Well, I'm sure I'll get to the bottom of this at some point. Maybe I just need more time. Maybe my fatigue and pain are just so strong that other feelings, specifically happy ones, aren't capable of manifesting themselves.

JUNE 7TH, 2015:
SEDATEPHOBIA

I'm running. I can't see what I'm running from. But I need to keep running. A brick wall. I keep running into a brick wall. I can't seem to get past it. I can't turn left or right.

Lines. In front of the brick wall are masses of squiggly lines thrashing violently. I'm scared.

And then I woke up. That dream was almost twenty years ago. But the effects of the dream have stayed with me and I finally figured out what it is.

Sort of.

I have anxiety. It's a mild form, I believe, but it's definitely anxiety. That dream, twenty years ago, was the start of it. I woke up that morning with a bout of anxiety, though at the age of eleven, I was too young to understand what it was. I asked my school counselor for help—the dream upset me so much that I thought I should tell someone—but she dismissed it.

Throughout the years, when I've been alone, whether trying to fall asleep or just wandering around my home, if it's silent, that dreadful feeling comes over me. I can start to see those chaotic squiggly lines again. I can't stop it; eyes open or eyes closed, I see them. That strange sight before my eyes, coupled with the knots in my stomach, paralyzes me. My senses heighten, noises seem far away yet close at the same time. And I wait. I wait for it to pass.

Having Sammy made me realize that I have anxiety, except of course, now it's worse. It comes stronger and more frequently, what with Witching Hour making a daily appearance. My anxiety has something to look forward to.

It's still a strange thing though, that it happens when it's quiet. I fear the silence. It's terribly loud. It forces me to sit in my own thoughts. My thoughts seem dark and I want to avoid them. I'd rather not be in my own head dealing with whatever is going on in there. I want to pretend that everything is fine. It's fine. Is this the kind of thing that you can "fake it till you make it"?

JUNE 22, 2015:
MAMA GOT HER GROOVE BACK

"What do I wear?! Nothing fits!" I yelled out, talking to myself as I attempted to zip up jeans that seemed to hate me. I was headed to an audition. My first one since well before Sammy was born (not a lot of roles for pregnant ladies out there). My agent recently emailed me an audition notice. But not just any audition. It was with a casting director who scares the bejesus out of me. He seems to treat the auditions like acting classes, making you come up with backstories for your character who is just pouring detergent or winning the lottery or walking behind the Massage Envy counter.

"There are four million people in LA, most of them actors, and most of them won't make it," he said the first day I met him, years before, when he dropped by an acting class to provide what I thought was going to be a pep talk. "Most of you won't either. It's just a fact," he went on to say.

A couple of years later, I landed an agent and began to see this casting director regularly for commercial auditions.

But now, oh God. Now, I'm so rusty. I've been out of practice for ages.

"Hi," I said to him when I walked in.

"Hi. Just put your things down over there and stand behind this tape and slate as usual please."

I put my bag down and walked in front of the camera, standing behind the blue piece of tape on the floor. My palms were sweaty. I was shaking. My jeans were so tight I could barely breathe (I had to drive to the audition with them unzipped). I looked around the room, seeing posters of famous plays and a pile of other actors' headshots and resumes. *So many of us after the same job.*

"Slate please," he said with his arms crossed after he adjusted the camera to my height.

I put on a fake smile. "Hi, I'm Suzanne Ziad and I'm with the Reynolds Agency."

"Good, now turn to your left, please...now to your right... and back to center." He panned the camera to my feet and pulled the camera up slowly, getting a full shot of my body. I may as well have been standing there naked, ridiculed for my changing body. A body that no longer belongs to me. This is my child's body now to feast, to keep awake.

Come to think of it, my mind isn't my own either. It belongs to no one, really. As my body that isn't mine moves along doing what is being asked of it, my mind seems to have been separated from my physical being. It's drifting around, hoping to find a more suitable host in which to reside. It hasn't found one yet, so it seems to be rotating around my body like a planet orbiting the sun.

My teeth were still mashed together in a fake smile as I began to say my lines, looking right into the camera. My voice shook. I have never felt so out of my element in front of a camera. I love the camera. It's where I shine. The knots in my stomach are usually butterflies during moments like this.

"I'm sorry," I said, stopping abruptly. "I haven't auditioned in a long time. I'm nervous. I just had a baby. Bit out of practice."

"That's okay. Take a minute. Reset. Then start again."

I closed my eyes and took a deep breath. *They want to see you succeed. They're looking for you to help make their commercial a success. You can do this. TALK SLOW.*

I opened my eyes, took one more deep breath, and began again.

"Oh my God, it was terrible. I'm so bad!" I cried to Kasim on the phone, having just walked out of the building where that man was no doubt laughing at how abysmal I was. "You know how my biggest problem is that I talk too fast? I somehow managed to talk even faster than I normally do. I would never hire me. And my breasts are killing me. I can feel the milk coming in and Sammy is thirty minutes away at your mom's."

"I'm sorry, love. I'm sure you were better than you think. You're your own worst critic. Grab a cup of coffee on your way home. That'll make you feel better," my husband said so lovingly. He hasn't figured out how to comfort me since the baby was born. He never seems to say the thing I need him to say. Probably because I don't know what I need him to say.

"I can't stop for coffee! I'm engorged. My milk is coming in. My breasts hurt right now just from my shirt touching my skin.

I don't have time to stop," I said quickly while unzipping my pants so I could cry and breathe at the same time.

"I'm sorry, love. Listen, I have a call in one minute. I love you."

"Bye," I said, hanging up quickly. I'm not even sure he caught my "bye."

I cried the entire way home. I don't know if it was because I was in physical pain or because my life as an actor was over. You're allowed to cry for more than one thing at a time, I suppose.

Two days later I got a callback. I couldn't believe they wanted me for a second audition. I was nervous, but when I walked into that same casting room, I was greeted by a few friendly faces from the producers of the commercial.

"Cillian!" I said, his name being the only one I could remember. I love Irish names, plus he has such a kind smile. It was hard to forget him.

"Hey!" he said. "We met at the film festival, right? You were pregnant?"

"Ha, yeah. That's me. It's good to see you guys."

"You too, Suzanne. Let's see what you got."

Feeling a little more relaxed, I turned to the camera and performed the lines that I had memorized.

I got the part. I couldn't believe it. My first time auditioning post baby and I got it! I can't tell you how good it feels. To know that I can still be me and not just a mom. I thought I couldn't be both.

And what a week it was. Nancy came over to watch the baby so I could go for a fitting; so fancy. Then the next day we began shooting. My agent told the production company in advance that I would have to take breaks now and then to pump. They were completely fine with it. I don't know why I thought it would be a problem.

The entire crew was so proficient that we finished a full day's work in half a day. I went back to the set the next day and we were all just as proficient. It was a wonderful week. I felt alive being with other humans and talking about the world of filmmaking.

I was the old Suz again. I missed her. It was nice to be with her again. I thought she had retired, Old Suz. I thought she had to leave to make room for New Suz, one I wasn't as comfortable with. The thing is, I really liked who I was. I thought I was pretty cool. I was happy in my own skin and happy in my mind. I was proud to be the person I grew up to be.

But then I became a mother. And all of that other stuff seemed to melt away. Most days I'm just a factory-farm cow whose only job is to nurse her young. I get sad every time Kasim leaves the house. Why does he get to go places and I don't? I know I chose to stay at home and take care of my baby. I know it's the best decision for our family. But I don't know how long I can do this.

And that's why this week was amazing. To be a mother and an actress. I can do anything; I can be anything.

JULY 7TH, 2015:
A HOLY PLACE

I'm so excited. I found the Mecca for mothers.

A few weeks ago Kristen came over to drop off some clothes for Sammy that no longer fit her now four-year-old boy, Chase. Hand-me-downs are a blessing.

"Oh, I've been meaning to ask you, have you heard of Modern Milk?" she asked while changing Chase's clothes. He had just had a pee accident. (A glimpse into my future, I suppose.)

"No. But that name is delightful. What is it?"

"Ah! It's so great. It's a workout place for Mamas. You can bring your baby into the class with you and do yoga and barre. It's a really cute place. I thought you'd like it. And it's a nice way to meet other mothers."

I've been thinking a lot lately of my judgement toward mothers now that I am one. I keep saying I want to still be me even though I'm a mom. And I seem reluctant to evolve into my new role. I can't be the only person that feels this way. Surely, these other mothers were interesting people before they became mothers and are still striving to stay that way. I've been thinking about all of this the wrong way. So when she mentioned this mama place, I decided to go.

"That sounds amazing. I would love that. Thank you. And thank you for the clothes. He's outgrowing his clothes so fast, I don't know how anyone keeps up with buying new clothes."

"Girl, between consignment stores and your friends wanting to donate their kids' clothes to you, you'll never need to buy new," she said as she handed Chase a sippy cup of juice. "And one last thing before I go. The best advice I ever got as a new mom: Don't be a hero. If someone offers to help you, take the help." That was the second time a mother said this to me—must be important. I logged that thought away somewhere near the front of my mind, in the same area I keep "call your grandparents on their birthdays" and "don't forget to shower."

Once Kristen had left, I looked up this Modern Milk place. They had a free yoga class the next day. It sounded perfect.

The following morning, Sammy and I were off to Modern Milk. When I walked in I was blown away. Everything was bright white, with teal and grey accents. You could tell it was a happy place. There was a sign painted on the wall in teal that said "Happy Mom, Happy Baby." The sign gave me pause. *Could it be that Sammy is so fussy because I am unhappy? Nothing seems to make him happy. And he still hasn't slept more than four hours at a time. If I fixed myself, would he be better? What am I supposed to fix?"*

I threw that thought aside.

"Hi. Can I help you?" a lovely blond woman with a warm

smile said to me as I walked up to the immaculate, white counter.

"Hi. Uh, I've never been here before. I heard there's a free yoga class you can take to try it out," I said while looking around at all the mothers and babies. There were women everywhere, clustered in groups and chatting while they all held their littles. Car seats were flung around the lobby. The sound of laughter from the mothers was mixing with crying from the babies and it overwhelmed me. But much to my surprise I didn't hate it.

"Unfortunately, the class is pretty full already," she said, pointing to a large window that looked into the yoga room. It was packed with yoga mats. A couple of women even took to having their mats half in, half out of the large, open doorway in order to participate.

"Oh. That's okay. I'll just look around then." She handed me a couple of papers with information on Modern Milk as well as a schedule of classes and events.

I really thought I would hate this place. I've developed such an aversion to mothers and babies. But this place had quite an effect on me. I was delighted to see mothers nursing their babies out in the open without a cover over the babies. The retail area was filled with all things mom and baby: swaddles, cute books, nursing bras, vitamins, iced coffee, healthy snacks. Did I mention iced coffee?

I looked at the information the woman handed me regarding the events that go on at Modern Milk. Just as Kristen said, they have yoga and barre. But they also have educational classes:

baby-led weaning (how to transition a baby from milk to solids without mashing food and spoon feeding-them. I didn't know that was a thing!), sleep-training classes, toddler discipline classes, breastfeeding classes, and even a dad class. I was blown away.

Even without taking the yoga class, I signed up as a member right then and there. I plan on coming every day for either barre or baby yoga. Baby Yoga. How cute is that?

I went home rejuvenated. I have a safe place to bring Sammy. A place where it doesn't matter if he cries or poops. I was in good company there. And maybe I will meet some cool women that just happen to be mothers. We'll see. I have a feeling that Modern Milk and I will be good friends.

JULY 8TH, 2015:
BABY MAMA BODY

This child does not sleep. What am I doing wrong? I'm frustrated with myself for not yet figuring out how to take care of him. He always seems so unhappy. Scratch that. Sometimes, he's fine. But it seems like more often than not, I can't make him happy. It's one thing when you and your baby don't seem to me meshing well. It's another when you're sleep deprived. Every emotion you experience seems heightened. It seems harder to control your state of mind when you just keep picturing your bed and wanting to be in it. Without him. Without anyone, really, so that you may wallow in your fatigue and misery.

But I'm a mother. The luxury of just taking a nap whenever I want to has flown out the window, along with my freedom. So I've decided to attempt to go about my business as best as I can. Right now, my new business is going to Modern Milk. I really want my body back. I'm uncomfortable in my own skin post baby. My entire body still aches in the morning. I don't stretch enough. I miss my pre-baby body. I'm sure it's unrealistic to think I'll ever look like I did when I was twenty-two but could I aim for twenty-seven years old? I was pretty hot three years ago and I didn't know it. Body dysmorphia is a real thing. I used to think I was fat. I was a size four. And I thought I was fucking fat. But my God, I was so far from that. What was I seeing? Even now, I continue to not like my body but I wonder, ten years from now am I going to look at a photo of myself post baby and think the same thing? "Oh honey, you looked fine, great even!" Why do we do this to ourselves? Nonetheless, everyone needs to exercise, to move their body. We all know it's good for the mind and soul as well as the body. So hop to, fat ass.

I threw on some yoga pants and a tank top with a built-in nursing bra and Sammy and I headed off to class. I found myself excited. I haven't been excited in a long time. I was headed to a place where I would get to talk to other adults and I'd get to work on my body. I had butterflies in my stomach. I've missed the butterflies. There's a fine line between butterflies and a knot— you know, the one when you're anxious or afraid. I'd be lying if I said I didn't enjoy the knot in the right circumstances—a just-missed car collision that didn't happen but your heart falls into your stomach; what a sensation that is. Once I know I'm out of danger, I let myself relish in that feeling. I suppose that's what makes adrenaline junkies do crazy things.

Lately it's just been sadness and anxiety and exhaustion and confusion and self-loathing deep in the bowels of my belly. The butterflies were a welcome change.

When I got there, I was greeted by the same lovely blond woman. Turns out she has a name. Allison. She showed me where to get a mat and I made my way into the barre room for class. A woman was already in there with her baby. She had her yoga mat laid out with her baby lying on a blanket at the top. I followed suit and put a small blanket down that I keep in my giant diaper bag and laid Sammy on top of it with a couple of toys. The new room and people and music were enough to stimulate him. He seemed positively mesmerized.

The workout itself was hard on me. It was hard on my body. Mentally, though, it was invigorating. If a move was difficult to do, I found myself wanting to do it more. But my body has been through a lot and the instructor told me to take it easy on my first day. About three quarters of the way through the class, Sammy needed to nurse. I pulled my yoga mat toward the wall so I could rest against it and I sat down right there and nursed him. It was wonderful not to have to leave the room. I even stretched along with the other women as Sammy ate. I knew this was the place for me. I didn't have to leave the room. I didn't have to feel awkward, wondering whether or not it was going to be weird to pull a breast out in the middle of the room. This was my safe space. A place of encouragement and understanding. A place where boobs are holy yet positively ordinary.

I also noticed the women. *How the hell did these women have time to blow dry their hair into those sleek waves? Is that a pedicure I see? When did they do that? How do they find the energy and time? God, I do not have my shit together, do I? Is this what all adult women do?*

I was happier when we walked back into the house a couple of hours later. I was aware of a significant shift in my mind and body. I felt physically lighter. My mind seemed to be pulsing with positive hormones. This is what I want to have more of. I'm tired of feeling tired and broken. I tried to take that boost with me through the rest of the day. And much to my surprise, it worked. When Kasim came home from work, Sammy and I were lying on the floor for tummy time. He walked in to see two smiling people. I know what he's been thinking. I'm not an idiot. It must be hard on him to come home and find a sad wife and screaming child. I can't imagine he looks forward to coming home, wondering what he's going to find when he gets there.

But today we were all happy. I took mental pictures of the three of us together, Sammy laughing for his father and Kasim smiling at me afterward. I even initiated sex. It's been a while since I've been the one to initiate.

"I really love Modern Milk," he said while we were getting back into bed after we had sex.

"You've never been there," I said, confused.

"Yeah, but it makes you happy and makes you want to have sex. So I love it," he said with a coy smile. I jokingly rolled my eyes at him as we both turned to face the same direction so he could hold me.

"Being a mother is really hard, Kasim," I admitted while I looked into the darkness, caught off guard that I was suddenly feeling sad.

"I know. I can see that. It's so easy for a dad. I just have to show up. You're doing all the work."

"If I had to do it all over again, I don't think I would," I said. It's a thought I've had since I realized I wasn't dreaming any of this and that I really do have a kid. It's a thought I'm ashamed of. But it's true.

He didn't respond but rather took a deep breath in and let it out slowly. I wondered if it was a sigh from frustration at the way I perceive our child. I started to wonder at my perception. I know I blame Sammy for the fact that I see myself as worthless. And I know it's not his fault. He didn't ask to be born. He's just this innocent, doe-eyed baby who so desperately needs my love. Why am I so reluctant to be what he needs me to be?

I listened for Kasim's breath to fall into a rhythmic state. I focused on it in an effort to fall asleep. But I couldn't. My mind was racing too much now. I began to fantasize about what life would have been like if I didn't get pregnant. It's a fantasy I've had dozens of times since April. It's a lovely fantasy filled with a smoking hot body on my part, dozens of acting gigs, and a potential move to LA. I picture Kasim and me at the Cannes Film Festival dressed to the nines or at Sundance wearing a cool T-shirt and jeans and boots.

Then there it was: that ache. That longing for something I've never had and would never have had in this alternate reality. The logical part of me knows this. But the reasonable part of me is no longer the part that prevails. It has been replaced with a strange sort of FOMO. Missing out on something I would never have experienced otherwise. But that doesn't matter.

A small voice, deep in the analytical part of my brain that

has seemed to shrink the last several months, is saying, *"You're an idiot. You just want an excuse to not be successful in your life. And now you get to blame your son. What kind of person does that?"*

And now I want to sleep so desperately. I want to not think about this anymore. It's too painful. I'm tired of the war that keeps raging in my mind.

JULY 18TH, 2015:
THERE WILL BE BLOOD

I'm thinking of creating a Public Service Announcement. No one else has done it and I think it's absolutely vital. If I did, it would go something like this:

(Unravels scroll in town square)

"Hear ye, hear ye! To expectant mothers: You have been told something. Something that I know now to be most untrue. I do not know if this lie is told to us as a form of hazing, but whatever the reason, I stand before you, humbly, to correct it.

"Ladies, it is quite possible that, although you are nursing your child, your period will come back to you.

(Hold for gasps, whispers, and jeering.)

"Again, I do not know why we are told that if you are nursing, you are unlikely to get it, but hear me, I am proof against this wicked lie!"

(Rolls scroll back up and pumps fist in the air.)

I can't believe I fell for this lie. It was such a nice one, though. Of course I would want to believe it. Nine months without a period was a wonderful part of pregnancy. It also seems like the logical thing. Surely our bodies wouldn't betray us by starting our cycles back up while we're still recovering from labor, dealing with emotional shit, sleep deprived, and nursing our babies until our nipples are raw. How much torture does one woman have to endure while sitting in her house with a person the size of a Boston Terrier as her only consistent companion? Surely not. It can't be.

Yet, here I am digging in the back of my closet and through small pockets in my purses for tampons.

I feel so betrayed by all the women who lied to me and by nature, who has bestowed this upon me. And who can blame me? My periods were always painful but I never dealt with mood swings. Until now, that is. (Can you call it a *swing* if you are firmly planted on the "pissed off" side of the pendulum?)

Just as I was angry-crying and rummaging through a box of Regular tampons, hoping a Super one was stashed inside, my husband walked in. And he was fucking whistling.

"Hey, love bug! What'chya doing on the floor?" he asked, annoyingly upbeat.

I stared daggers at him. No doubt foam was seeping from the side of my mouth. There will be blood tonight, indeed.

JULY 23RD, 2015:
HOME

Home is where the heart is. Home is where you are the happiest. Home is through that beautiful silver Arch that stands tall and proud over the Mississippi River. I'm home.

Kasim had a business meeting in St. Louis, so I shamelessly took advantage and made a family trip out of it. I'm so happy to be back in my old stomping grounds. Every street holds a beautiful childhood memory. I feel at peace here.

This afternoon, while Kasim was off speaking at a marketing event, Sammy and I went to my favorite place in the city, Forest Park, to meet my best friend, Sofia. Forest Park is a woodland haven for the local urban population. Aside from the beautiful greenery, it's filled with free arts and culture for everyone. I spent years running around this place at the outdoor theater, the art museum, the zoo, the science center...the list goes on. It's my happy place.

"Aaaahh!" We both screamed as we hugged each other. We haven't lived in the same city since college. Seeing each other is rare. Our relationship has survived thanks to the technology gods who created a little thing called text messaging. Strangely, it was weird using my voice to talk to her. That's not how we communicate.

"I missed you so much," I said with the biggest smile on my face.

"I missed you too," she said to me though she was already kneeling down to look at Sammy in his stroller. "Hi, my little nephew," she said to him as he looked at her like a deer in the headlights. She hasn't changed a bit since I last saw her, three years ago. She's tall (which never changes but always makes me jealous), blond, and has beautiful curves and an infectious, bright smile—she's a real Russian beauty.

"Sammy, this is Khalto Sofia," I said to him. "So-Fia," I said slowly as I pointed to her.

"How do you say aunt?" she asked. "Khal-too," I said, now slowly pronouncing it for her.

Sofia speaks four languages and is eager to keep learning. As we walked through the park we spent a few minutes working on the pronunciation of Arabic words she's been working on. Sammy was taking in the view and wasn't a bother at all. Forest Park is so magical it soothes the fussiest of babies.

"So," Sofia began, shifting our language lesson to something different. "How are you? Honestly."

"Um," I said, trying to buy time. She wasn't the kind of person in my life I had to be fake with. She was no stranger to darkness and I knew I could say whatever I needed to say.

"I don't really know how I am. Being a mom sucks, honestly. I'm going through the normal stuff they tell you about:

exhaustion, nipple pain, randomly crying, abdominal pain, etc., but it hasn't gotten any better. It hasn't lightened up at all. My anxiety is through the roof. I didn't even know I had anxiety! I've also got this really heavy feeling almost all of the time. I have moments of happiness. Sometimes, Sammy will do something so cute and I'll just burst with joy. But most of the time, I'm like Pig-Pen from Charlie Brown—except instead of a cloud of dirt following him around, it's a cloud of sadness. I only just thought of that metaphor. Most of the time I've been likening it to a Dementor."

"Ah, that makes sense. Good example," she said. I appreciated her Harry Potter knowledge. I liked not having to explain it any further because J.K. Rowling paints the picture so beautifully.

And as if she were reading my thoughts, she said, "You know what the Dementors are?"

"Uh, yeah. You forgot who you're talking to," I said, trying to put a little humor into the conversation.

"No, I mean, what they represented to Rowling. She suffered from depression. And the Dementors were her characterization of what depression looks like and what it can do to a person."

I stopped in my tracks. "Depression?"

"It's possible," she said gently. "Do you think you could be depressed? Postpartum depression?"

Thankfully, I eyed a bench just a few feet away. I walked to it and sat down. Sofia sat down next to me. I looked at the baby, who had finally fallen asleep. I lowered his little hat a bit to block the sun so he could sleep without disruption. We sat in silence for a bit.

"I'm depressed?" I finally managed to get out.

"I don't know if you are. But it's possible. You're describing depression. I've never had postpartum depression, but I do suffer from depression and what you're experiencing is very similar to what I experience, except I don't have a kid to take care of as I'm falling apart." I thought back on the many dark moments she's had where I either in person or digitally held her hand. She would explain that depression made her not think clearly, that it was hard to see your way out of it, that even though you knew the dark moment was temporary, you never thought the pain would go away.

"But I've never been depressed before," I said, staring out at the lake and the happy people rowing on it. I hated them for looking so content.

"I know you haven't. But you've also never had a kid before. Postpartum depression is sort of its own beast. It's a direct response to having a child. It's nothing to be ashamed of," she said kindly.

"No, it's not that. It's just that this explains a lot. I thought that this was my new life. That being a mother is the worst thing that could ever happen to a woman. I thought this was my new normal. I didn't realize I might be in a temporary postpartum state of depression." I was more thinking out loud than talking to Sofia at this point. But then I remembered she was there. I turned to her. "Wait, this is temporary, right?"

"I don't know. I would assume so; it's called "postpartum."
Maybe now that you've potentially identified it, you can start to
work on it," she said, also seemingly thinking out loud.

"How do you work on depression?" I wondered. I started
to wonder if it's something you cured with a pill, which didn't
sound appealing to me. Maybe it's through therapy. But am I
ready to admit that something is wrong?

"I don't know." She looked at me, helpless. She was the one
who has experienced this for years but was unable to answer
the question I most needed answered. I burst out laughing.
She looked at me, stunned for a brief moment, and then began
to laugh with me. Tears began streaming down my face and I
realized that I was no longer laughing, but crying. Sofia put her
arm around me and didn't say another word. She just let me
cry.

We got up and walked around the park, reminiscing about
times gone by in this beautiful place. I pointed to Art Hill,
where I sat with my college boyfriend, where I fell in love with
him. I smiled at this memory. It was nice to think of a time in
my life when I had adult freedom but no adult responsibility.
I just got to be an idealistic twenty-one-year-old, sitting with a
hot boy I met in a college class, talking about all the ways we
would change the world.

We walked past the grassy patch where Shakespeare in the
Park was held each summer—where Sofia and I and a few
others would go and enjoy good theater, further fueling my
desire to act.

In that time, I almost forgot about my newly discovered issue. As we said our goodbyes and I put Sammy back in the rental car, the Dementors swarmed me. My stomach started to hurt, and I wanted to throw up. I wish I could throw up. Maybe it would make everything better.

Sofia and I hugged one more time. "You're going to be fine. You can tell me anything, okay? No matter how dark. No judgement here."

"Yeah, okay. Thanks," I said as I pulled away from our embrace. "See you soon, Inshallah." I blew a kiss goodbye as I drove away in silence, taking in my revelation.

It took four months, a four-hour flight and a forty-five-minute drive to find out that I have postpartum depression. There is something poetic and right about the fact that I learned this while sitting with my best friend in my favorite park, in the city that I love the most, the place that makes me happy, the place that I call home.

JULY 30TH, 2015:
NOT YET

One might think that by now I would have told Kasim about what's going on. Nope. I mulled it over for a week. I have thousands of conversations in my head that never need to see the light of day. I can resolve a problem I have with someone without them being any the wiser, as I've done it all in my mind. It's much easier than confronting the person. Is it healthier? No. Do I do it anyway because I'm terrified to talk about all of this? Yup.

I know Kasim has been frustrated and probably annoyed with my response to motherhood. We haven't talked about it because I think he's walking on eggshells around me. In the past I have struggled with any sort of constructive criticism from him. He's such a go-getter. Anything he wants to do, he does it, and does it well. He's building a system of habits that makes him a machine. It's quite impressive. But the more impressive he gets, the smaller I feel. That's not on him. It's on me and how I perceive myself. Nonetheless, it can be hard to talk to him about my own insecurities.

I was having a particularly bad day. I loved being back in St. Louis. I didn't realize how much I missed home until our plane landed and the flight attendant said, "Welcome to St. Louis." Such beautiful words. For a moment just then I resented my parents for moving us out of St. Louis. I was happy there. Why did I have to leave it? Then I remembered what I found in Phoenix—the love of my life, the father of the baby that I now hold in my arms.

On the flight back to Phoenix, I nursed Sammy as the plane was taking off in order to help his little ears deal with the altitude. As we flew away from my childhood home, it was like someone was pulling my insides out. It ached. Walking around Forest Park with my best friend, I was flooded with memories of my favorite moments: Shakespeare in the Park every Memorial Day evening, the African Festival, romantic dates with boys who knew that the best place to take a girl was Art Hill in Forest Park. I smiled as I thought about those moments, but it was a painful smile.

Nostalgia is a tricky business. I tend to live a nostalgic life, always wishing for things that are no longer, whether it's wishing I lived in a different time that I have never experienced but have romanticized (enter *Midnight in Paris* here), or wanting to go back to my college days, which, to this day, are full of the most fun times I have ever had.

I'm not an idiot. I know I can't keep thinking like this. I can't help it. I find myself to be quite comfortable when I'm not living in the present moment. Anxiety, in its distilled form, is fear of the future. So, yes, I enjoy living in a place that no longer exists but is very alive in my mind.

"Are you okay?" Kasim asked me on the drive home from the airport as I stared out the window, not talking.

"Yeah, of course. I'm fine. I was just sad to leave. It was nice to be back there," I said softly. I wasn't ready to tell him that I thought I had postpartum depression. But it's best to keep a lie as close to the truth as possible. And I was sad to leave. And it was, indeed, nice to be back there. So, technically, I was being truthful. I felt a pang of guilt, the kind you get when you've lied to your Sunday School teacher.

He didn't say anything in reply. I turned to look at him. He had that look on his face that I know very well. If you didn't know him, you would say he was expressionless. But that lack of expression is his way of suppressing his frustration. Is he frustrated because I'm sad? Or does he know I'm not telling him everything? The world may never know.

I thought knowing that I was depressed would make me less depressed because I now know the source of my sadness. But it wasn't the case. I fell further into depression. I'm depressed that I'm depressed, if that makes any sense—what a fucking catch-22. I usually try to forget about it by distracting myself. And the distractions aren't always conscious. I don't say to myself, "Okay, you're sad. So why don't you watch an episode of *Friends* and forget about your troubles?" I just seem to forget that I'm in a temporary state of depression and I go about doing things around the house. My natural state is one of gratitude and contentment and sometimes it seems that part of me is trying to make its way back to the surface where it used to reside. When you're the daughter of immigrant parents who came here to give their kids a better life, it's very easy to see how good you have it. Gratitude was a part of our upbringing.

The thing about depression—at least for me—is that it comes in waves. There is always a dark cloud, hovering near you, slowly filling up with dark thoughts, then suddenly, out of the blue, you're drenched in this flash flood. Sometimes you can see it coming, but other times, it's as if it purposely sneaks up on you—a trojan horse disguised as something trivial like not having cucumber juice and suddenly the world is bleak, your body is in pain, you feel so heavy you cannot possibly move. But you have to move. Your baby needs you. He wants to eat, he wants to play, he wants your love. Where will you get that energy and love from? It's not in you to give. It's been stolen, if it was ever there in the first place, by an invisible entity that is hellbent on your destruction. Dementors are invisible to some people. How do you fight something you cannot see?

But you move forward anyway, you get distracted with your tasks, your child does something cute, you FaceTime with your sister and she tells you something funny, and slowly, the flood around you evaporates, leaving you with just a puddle for now. Things slowly drift back to your current version of normal and you continue about your business. Meanwhile, there's that bloody cloud, still near you, still finding things to fill itself with for the next storm.

"Hey, I'm gonna be home late again tonight," Kasim said

over the phone. "I was on calls all day and haven't gotten any actual work done. Is that okay?"

"Sure, of course," I said, not at all meaning it. But what can I do? Tell him that I need him? Tell him that my mental health is fraying and I need him to take care of me? Yeah, I don't know how to do that. "Just give me a thirty-minute heads up so I can have dinner ready for you when you get back," I said instead.

"Okay, love you, love bug."

When he came home, the house was quiet and clean. I was lying on the couch watching *Friends* on my iPad. Sammy had just fallen asleep but I wasn't really in the mood to sleep yet. I needed to decompress. And nothing helps me decompress more than Chandler Bing, bless him. When you're watching a show you have seen hundreds of times, you don't have to focus too much and you know what's coming. In this case, I look forward to Chandler's funny lines and even chuckle at times. Maybe it's because I really need to laugh. Or maybe he's just that good.

I didn't greet him when he got home. Unless you can call "Hey" a greeting while my head was still on the pillow. I hated being home alone with Sammy. I hated dealing with Witching Hour alone, bathing him alone, playing with him alone, putting him to sleep alone, soothing him back to sleep alone. Alone.

"What's wrong?" he said, walking back into the living room after he made himself a plate of food.

"I hate doing the bedtime routine alone. He's so cranky. He

never stops crying. And I don't know what I'm doing wrong. You've been working late a lot and I just hate doing all of this alone. I need you home more. You have to be here to help me."

He was silent for a minute. No doubt constructing his words in the manner that was the most refined and void of emotion. Then, finally, he spoke.

"I don't know what to do here. Running your own company is hard. I'm responsible for so many families, who rely on me for their income. I don't have the time or luxury to step away whenever you need me. I'm sorry if that's harsh. I don't intend for it to be. But we both have roles here. I'm home on the weekends and I don't go into work until 9, so you have me in the mornings.

"Maybe you can get up early, feed Sammy, and go get a cup of coffee and read at Starbucks for a bit before I have to go to work. And if you need a break on the weekends and you just wanna get away, we can figure that out too, I guess."

He sounded cold. It was like he was trying so hard to stay neutral. Maybe these small getaways would help. Maybe they wouldn't. Right now, my problem doesn't seem like it could be helped with overpriced coffee. This was bigger. I was having a mental health crisis. But he didn't know that. This was the most opportune time to tell him. He was looking at me, waiting for my response. He needed to know. *He can't help you like this. You're not giving him a chance to be the amazing, supportive husband he's always been. Just say it. I'm depressed. I have depression. I need help.*

"A coffee break sounds nice. Maybe I could go tomorrow morning?" I was a fucking chicken.

"Of course, lovebug." He kissed me on the cheek and got up. He walked over to the kitchen. "Dinner smells good."

I didn't respond. I pressed play on the iPad and lay there, tears streaming down my face.

AUGUST 3RD, 2015:
SHE'S SO STUPID

My friend John invited me to be a part of this philanthropy group. You pay a certain amount of money to join and these non-profits in the area then put up a proposal as to why they should receive funding, the benefit they provide to the community, etc. John is allowed to have a plus one, as it were, on the team, so he invited me. The last few months, once a month, we have had meetings where the non-profits get to pitch their ideas. Tonight was the night that we declared the winners. It was really lovely. The organization rented out this beautiful theater where they were to do that fun thing that Ellen does where she hands a lucky person a giant check.

So I sat in one of the back rows and enjoyed the adult, alone time. I went a bit early because I was dying to get out of the house and start my evening alone. Naturally, I brought a book with me. As I sat there reading *Mistborn* (a fantasy fiction series about a badass female—my favorite kind of story), I looked up and saw a very cool woman slowly scooching her way toward me. It took a moment to recognize her as I was too awed by her look. She had thick, straight, blond hair, gorgeous bronze skin; she was tall, even more so in her black stilettos; and she wore a T-shirt that managed to drape on her body, perfectly sitting on the top of her jeans. After I gave her the typical once over, I looked back in her face and recognized the mole above her lip. It was Rachel, the coolest woman in Phoenix. She runs a non-profit that supports startups and she hosts a yearly party called "Cool People, Cool Shit," where, you guessed it, she finds all the coolest people around who are doing the coolest shit, and puts them all in a room together to meet. It's brilliant. I watched her coming closer and thought about how cool she was and how lucky she was not to have tied herself down to a baby. She was living the good life. I smiled as she approached, her face slowly lighting up as she, too, recognized me.

"Rachel! Hi!" I said, standing up to greet her.

"Suzanne! Hi! It's really nice to see you." We hugged. Ugh, even the way she hugs is cool. I stood in the tight aisle between theater seats clutching my book to my chest, shifting from foot to foot, trying not to fall over.

"Is this seat taken?" She took the seat next to me. Before we had a chance to strike up a conversation where I would desperately attempt to act cooler than I am, the lights dimmed and the show started.

I wasn't paying attention to the show. I kept thinking about Rachel and her baby-free life. What a cool life she chose to have: helping people support themselves through innovative start-ups, taking meetings all over the city. If memory serves, I'm pretty sure she won one of those 30 under 30 awards for her entrepreneurial successes. My personal heavy cloud was now looming over my head, drizzling. I had chosen the wrong path in life, and here was Rachel, sitting next to me, reminding me of my choices, of my mistakes.

I got through the show as best as I could. Afterward, there was a cocktail hour in the lobby where we would congratulate the winners and have, wait for it, mashed potato martinis. Easily the best part of the night. Mashed potatoes with a buffet of toppings that didn't occur to you could belong on mashed potatoes, served in martini glasses. I mean, come on. That's a good time. As I wandered around with my martini glass and plastic spoon, scooping up mashed potatoes and gravy, Rachel and I bumped into each other.

"Hi, again!" she said. I noticed she had no Mashed Potato Martini in hand. Of course not. She's way too cool to be stuffing her face with complex carbohydrates. I casually put mine down on the cocktail table we were standing next to.

"Hey! I didn't know you would be here, it was a nice surprise."

"Oh yeah, I know the organizers. It's a small town."

"Yeah, it does seem that way, doesn't it? For as big as Phoenix is, it's pretty small."

"So, what's new? What have you been up to?" she asked.

"Oh, nothing. I had a baby this year, so I've been pretty busy with that. What about you?" I said, not wanting to talk about me and the baby.

"Oh, congratulations! That's wonderful!" she said, as expected. Honestly, I could predict people's responses down to the exclamation point. Before she could start asking me more on this topic, I moved on.

"What about you? What's going on in your world?"

"Actually, my boyfriend and I are moving to Northern California to be close to family. We're not telling people yet, but I'm pregnant." She grabbed my wrist and lowered her voice at the last part. She was sharing this with me, a fellow mother. I was to be her confidant this evening. I was to understand her better than anyone here, new mother to new mother.

I was flabbergasted. What an idiot. How could she do this? How could she throw away her cool life like this? And to be excited about it. It was appalling. But you can't tell people this. I'd sound insane. So, of course, let's play-act.

"Aw, that's great! Congratulations!" I said, attempting to really hit those exclamation points in a show of solidarity with this person who has no idea how hard it's going to be or how she's essentially just ruined her entire life. I suddenly noticed that I had my Mashed Potato Martini back in hand.

And then, do you know what we did? We talked about nursing bras for the rest of the conversation. I don't even know how it happened, but our conversation ended with me promising to email her the company that makes the bras I like the most. I was one of *those* women now. How did that end up happening? She's been pregnant for three seconds and immediately this is what we talk about. A couple of hours ago, I was watching her walk toward my seat in the theater and I was jealous of her freedom. Now she is to be chained. Honestly, how disappointing.

I said goodbye to Rachel and left soon afterward. I drove home confused, in deep thought about it all. If someone as put together and as successful as she is, can make room in her life for a child, could I? Then again, I'm not as successful. I'm a former activist/wannabe actor who has no idea where she is going in life. And then I chose to add a baby into that mix. So is it different for her?

It seems silly to be so bothered by this. I normally try not to let emotion really play a part in my decision-making. I can't wrap my mind around why I'm so upset about this. It's almost like I'm grieving for her and her stupid mistake.

AUGUST 8TH, 2015:
THE RING

You know that ring I've been wearing for about six years? The masks of Thalia and Melpomene, otherwise known as Comedy and Tragedy? I got it in LA at a random jewelry stand. I love it more than any other piece of jewelry. I love it more than my wedding ring. I don't really wear my wedding ring. I suppose I couldn't if I wanted to, it doesn't fit my now pudgier finger. After the excitement of the shiny diamond wore off, I realized I'm not the type of person who wants to wear a wedding ring. I didn't really appreciate what it meant. I know you can say it's a symbol of our love, our commitment to each other. But I don't see it that way. It's a "Hey Pal, back off, I'm married, don't even look at me." And that's no fun. Anyway, I digress.

I had this nervous tick where I moved my Mask ring up to my knuckle and bent my knuckle. I didn't realize I was doing it. Sometime while I was pregnant, the ring cracked in half, separating the two faces. I was pretty bummed out but too tired to feel anything too strongly. It's funny to think I can cry over missing cucumber juice, but a piece of jewelry that has significance to me, that I wear every day no matter what, I don't have the energy to be sad about. I wish I could work me out.

Well, anyway, let's not digress again and go down that rabbit hole. I don't have the energy for that either.

It was about 7 p.m. last night and I had just gotten Sammy to sleep. I knew he was going to be up soon. I had about two or three hours before the milk service began. It had been a rough day with Sammy. My nipples were raw from his cluster feeding, we were both cranky, and I wanted to take this opportunity to sleep. I put him in his bassinet and slipped into my own bed right next to him. As I was lying down, tears, I think from just pure mental and bodily fatigue, started to fall down the side of my face onto my pillow. Out of the blue, Kasim came to my side of the bed, pulled my left hand out from under the sheet, and slipped a new, intact, Thalia and Melpomene right onto my middle finger. The light from the hallway was just enough that I could see what it was. I couldn't lift my head up off the pillow. The fatigue, mixed with his sweet gesture, caused some sort of weird gravitational pull and I couldn't lift myself to thank him. But my mouth worked.

"Habibi. It's wonderful. It's even nicer than the old one. Thank you," I said through quiet tears.

"What's wrong, love bug?"

"Nothing," I lied. "I'm just tired." Which I suppose fixed the lie. I was tired. Tired in my body, in my brain, in my soul, in my wherever it's possible to be tired.

"Go to sleep, then," he said, moving the hair out of my face. He kissed me on the cheek and walked away.

It seems I am both Thalia and Melpomene. Swinging back and forth between comedy and tragedy, trying to land on just one, even if it was tragedy. At least that way, I would know how I'm feeling. The constant back and forth is giving me whiplash.

"Kasim," I quietly called out, afraid to wake up the baby. "I love you."

"Love you too, lovebug."

Love. I'm finding that I don't know if I understand that word. Since Sammy, I have questioned what it means.

One random day, not long ago, I told Sammy I loved him. At that moment it dawned on me: What is love? I think I love him, but not like I love Kasim or my parents or my friends or Adele or my first car or French fries. I started to wonder what that word really means. Loving a child, they say, is the ultimate love. I know I would die for my child, I would do anything I had to do to ensure that he is safe and healthy and free from harm. Every mother in the animal world would do the same. So is love just instinct, just biology? I wonder if it means as much if it's just a default mechanism built into my DNA to ensure our survival. It bothers me that I can't figure it out. I want to love for the right reasons, I want to love because I choose to love. I want to love myself and be loved in return. You know when you say a word over and over it starts to sound funny?

Love—the word seems to have lost all meaning.

AUGUST 9TH, 2015:
THE EXCELLENCE IN BABYSITTING AWARD

"Suck in just a little more, Suz!"

"Selwa! I am!" I yelled back at my sister, who was helping me squeeze into a dress of hers. It was a soft, mint-green dress that fell straight down to my toes with a sexy open back. And pockets.

Tonight was the Excellence in Design award show. A celebration of the region's interior designers. Saeed, as a vendor in the design industry, was a sponsor every year and always invited us along. Every year, we enjoyed a night out—fancy food at a fancy hotel, dressing up in black tie attire, sleeping over at the hotel, and waking up the next morning for breakfast with Saeed and his staff. Honestly, any excuse to dress up and I'm there. Plus, like I said before, the dress has pockets.

Sammy is only a few months old and I knew I couldn't be away from him for too long. My sisters, Selwa and Sandy, offered to watch him in our hotel room while we attended the event downstairs.

"Ready?" Kasim asked, popping back into the hotel after a quick run-through before the show started.

"She's ready. Are you excited to be the MC?" Selwa asked Kasim as she was straightening the back of my dress for me. Sometimes I like to pretend I'm famous and Selwa is my personal stylist and makeup artist. I just stand there and she makes me pretty. If I do ever get famous, I think I'll make her quit her job and offer her a shit ton of money to just follow me around and keep me looking fabulous. That's a job, right?

"Yup. Any excuse to be on stage," he said, taking a last look in the mirror.

"You two are made for each other," Selwa said as she watched us preening in the mirror.

Kasim and I headed downstairs in the Phoenician Hotel for our adult night. When we entered the ballroom, Kasim went to the stage and I made my way over to Saeed's table.

"You look lovely, my child," Saeed said to me as he got up to give me a hug.

"Thanks, Ami," I said, wondering how I was going to sit down without the zipper breaking or coming undone.

Even with that horrific thought in my head, I still grabbed the bread basket and butter. I sighed as I bit into the warm, buttery roll. If I could only ever eat one thing again: Bread. And cheese. Cheese and bread. But that's it.

The evening started as it always does with an introduction from the president of the interior design organization. As I'm not in the organization and am only there for the free food and chance to put on a dress, I usually find myself to be a bit bored with the entire production. My only job there is to be Kasim's cheerleader and rudely shush people who are rudely talking and not listening to the hot MC speak.

After what felt like seventeen hours, I heard my phone make its usual dinging noise, telling me that someone had texted me. The text was from Selwa.

"Sammy won't stop crying. I'm so sorry. I don't know what to do. I've tried everything. Can you come up, please?"

I took one more bite of my food and raced upstairs to relieve my baby sisters from what I can only assume was the best form of birth control I could think of.

My God, I can hear him from the elevator. I opened the hotel door to find Selwa holding him on the balcony. I half wondered if she was considering throwing either the baby or herself over the railing.

"I'm so sorry, Suz. He hasn't stopped this entire time. He won't take a bottle. I changed him. I've been playing with him. I don't know what to do."

I took my child from my sister's arms and held him to my chest. "It's okay. I was pretty sure he wasn't going to cooperate. For whatever reason, he loves his mama." The look on her face mirrored my own, the face that I have had permanently fixed on since Sammy was born.

I took off my heels, falling closer to the earth, and sat on the bed in a comfortable position to feed Sammy. It was quiet now. I could see the fatigue in Selwa's face as well as Sandy's annoyed look. She hates loud noises. When the room was dead silent, Selwa sighed in relief. I know that sigh. Her ears must have been ringing from his incessant screaming. She must have been frustrated out of her mind for not knowing how to make him happy. A feeling I know all too well. And I don't wish it on anyone, let alone my baby sister.

"Jesus Christ, I am never having children," she said as she plopped herself down on a chair. "How do you do this all the time?" *Birth control for my college-age sister. Silver Lining.*

"I don't know, but it sucks. A lot. I kinda hate it."

"I don't blame you."

Selwa told me to go back downstairs once Sammy was fed. But I couldn't. I didn't think I should leave Sammy again, even if he was asleep. And I just wasn't up for it anymore. He'd bummed me out. This isn't the first or second time something has been cut short because no one can handle the screaming infant. Maybe this is just my life now.

How many times have I gone to family dinners and ended up isolating myself in someone's room while I nurse? Everybody seems to forget I was even there. You'd think someone would come looking for me.

"Hey, wasn't Suz just here?" Relative A might ask.

"Oh yeah. Where'd she go?" asks Relative B.

"She's feeding the baby," Relative C, D, E, F, or G would reply.

And then a few of the letters would find me and keep me company. But they often don't. They're all excited to see each other after some time apart—eating, talking loudly, drinking, laughing. Who would wanna slip away into a room tucked as far away from the lovely madness as possible while being forced to whisper lest the baby wake up?

Maybe I don't get a life outside of Sammy anymore. Maybe, from now, it's just me and him. God, what a horrid thought. What happened to that village everyone talks about? I'm alone.

AUGUST 10, 2015:
GREAT SCOTT!

Okay, this has happened so many times that it's actually starting to get weird.

Sometimes, because I'm bored out of my damn mind, Sammy and I will go to Target. It's too hot to do much outdoors. And with a baby, you always need something from Target. Or you can pretend that you do, so you can get out of the house. But every time I go, the strangest thing happens.

There I am, standing in one of the baby aisles, looking for organic shampoo or diapers or wipes or a cute little pajama onesie covered in dinosaurs, and someone else in the aisle, someone who is well beyond the years of early parenthood, will inevitably say, "Enjoy it. It goes by fast." It's the same exact two sentences. In that order. Every time. "Enjoy it. It goes by fast." I smile and say, "Yeah." Because what am I supposed to say? "No, pushy stranger. This has been the most drawn out, most miserable time of my life. I hate every minute of this and cannot wait until I'm further into the future when he's like ten years old and is capable of talking to me like a normal person and isn't draining me of all of my resources." Or better yet, "I kinda, sorta wish that I didn't start all this to begin with and that it's just a bad dream that I will, if God has any sympathy, wake me up from."

I really want to say that. But I don't. The most interesting part is the look on all of their faces. It's frantic. It's in pain. They seem to have really felt this, that it goes by fast and they didn't enjoy it enough, and as good humans, they desperately want to save strangers from the same fate. In fact, it is their mission on this earth to make sure that the unhappy woman in aisle 12D doesn't make the same mistake, doesn't take this time for granted, sees the beauty in it, and truly lives in the moment, in this time that can never happen again, a time that will be looked upon later with such fondness. You just know that they're hoping the government has a secret time machine and they can find a way to go back and correct this grave error.

Yeah, bullshit. These people are nuts. I'm just lucky I'm still alive and can drive to the store. And wear a shirt. (Nursing makes you not want to wear a top. What's the point when you have to remove it every ten seconds?)

I know they are well-intentioned people. But I'm in no position to receive this pearl of wisdom. I don't want it.

SEPTEMBER 4, 2015:
THE BIRTHDAY THAT WASN'T

I turned thirty yesterday. Hitting a new decade is interesting, particularly this one. I wonder if I will be taken more seriously in my thirties. I wasn't ever sure if I was taken seriously in my twenties. I keep telling Kasim that no one listens to me on account of I'm too adorable.

Not as much the last couple of years, but for most of my twenties, I was a very typical idealist. I think I was who you are supposed to be at that age—easily excited, hopeful about life, convinced you can single-handedly save the planet. Then real life sets in and you change, you seem calmer, more realistic, and, sadly, slightly jaded. Wait, do you? Is that all of us? Is that part of the many phases of human development?

Shakespeare so beautifully said, "One man in his time plays many parts, his act being seven ages..." From a young, excited lover, to a soldier who is quick to go to battle (this would be the twenties, idealist phase, surely), then the justice, "full of wise saws and modern instances."

Have I just entered into the wise saws and modern instances act? Someone who maybe has seen a little bit of life and is changed by it in a way that is natural to the order of a human's existence?

If it is, I think it's a good thing. In my twenties, particularly in college, with all my human rights buddies around me, talking about how we were going to change the world, we didn't have a clue what that looked like, we just had all the energy in the world to do it. Perhaps in your thirties, now you know what you're really capable of, how far you are actually willing to go to get what you want and how to realistically set about doing it.

I remember when I used to think thirty was old. Thirty was when your life was over and you shouldn't even bother trying anymore. It's funny to think how we demonize age. I still have a good seventy years left if my grandparents are any indication of my mortality.

Sometimes when I notice how much time has passed me by, I consider how for the first nineteen years or so of my life, I just wandered around, living, yes, but not aware of my existence. When you're a child, you don't ponder these things, you just live. What a beautiful thing. I've only really been awake for a decade, only an adult for such a short amount of time, with so many years to go. It does make me sad, though, to think we spend more time as adults than we do as children. If there is any time of life to really make the most of, it's the fleeting chapter of childhood. Of course, you can't tell a kid that. They're too busy living.

Every birthday, I, like so many, take the time to evaluate where I am in my life and where I want to be headed. This year is different. This year, I'm a mother. My thoughts are not just about me, but about my little family, my nucleus. I haven't mentally prepared for how to prepare for the future when I have more than myself to think about. I suppose, since I'm writing in my journal, musing, this is me attempting to think about it. But all I can think about is just trying to survive, trying to get over the shell shock of becoming a mother. I hate when people use war terminology to describe things in their own lives that are far less dangerous than being murdered by a foreign enemy, but I can't think of anything else to describe the last five months other than complete shock, please forgive the expression.

So here's to thirty. Maybe the next decade will be one full of hope, a few good surprises, and a lot of love.

*Oh my gosh! All that stuff I just wrote isn't why I grabbed my journal tonight. I wanted to write down that I cried all day yesterday for no reason, Kasim went to lunch with his dad on my birthday and that pissed me off, but I never told him, because I don't know how to tell him when I'm sad or mad, and that we attempted to go to a dinner theater, but before the curtain opened, my mother called me, telling me to come pick up my kid because he won't stop crying, then of course by the time we got to my parents' house, Sammy had worn himself out and was asleep. Right. That was my day.

SEPTEMBER 9TH, 2015:
WHAT ARE THE RULES?

When Kasim and I got married, we fell into very traditional gender roles, but it worked for us. I had a part-time job at Starbucks so I was home a lot. He ran his own company and worked more than most humans. I was fine doing all the domestic work. It made sense. But what happens after you have a child? I'm not talking about who cleans the bathroom now. I'm home with the baby, and again, I don't mind doing the housework. I have the time.

My job is to be the primary caretaker. I'm the stay-at-home parent. But you don't get to clock out of parenting, take a sick day, get rewarded for overtime, decide you want to ignore the call of your crying baby. My job, it seems, is to be with the child 24/7. But when did we decide that?

"Hey, the weather is getting better and John is putting the volleyball tournament back together," Kasim said one night recently while we were getting ready for bed. I was standing there naked, trying to get used to my strange new body. I've been feeling stronger since going to barre at Modern Milk three days a week. I stand there a lot analyzing the work I've been doing.

"Oh, are you gonna play again?" I asked, watching my very skinny husband put on his boxers.

"Yeah. You don't mind, do you? It's just once a week. Wednesday nights. I have time to come home and eat first. It's not until the sun sets."

Right. So he's out of the house all day. He'll come home to a meal that I've prepared for him as I've waited all day for him to come home. He'll play with the kid for a few minutes, then run off to go play with his friends. While I do what, exactly? Oh, that's right, not have a social life. Got it.

"Yeah. That's fine. I'm not gonna tell you no, Kasim. I'm not your mother." Mercifully, Sammy cried from his crib. I threw on a robe and headed off to do my job. I went to Sammy's room to find that he managed to unwrap himself from his swaddle and was now agitated and very awake.

"Hello, habibi. What did you do?" I said in my sweet Mama voice even though I was mad. But at this point, I wasn't mad at Sammy like I usually am. My anger, for once, wasn't directed toward him. I was mad at Kasim. I picked up Sammy and walked over to the rocking chair on the other side of his room and settled in to comfort-nurse him. *Maybe I could stay here long enough for Kasim to get in bed and fall asleep so I don't have to talk to him*, I thought to myself. I hummed an Adele tune[3] (I hate lullabies) and let my mind wander.

Kasim goes to yoga before work; he meets up with friends occasionally, on a Saturday morning for some coffee or evening

---

3 All hail Adele and her album *19*.

drinks with his business mentor. It's not even a question of if he's able to. He just gets to do it. He has freedom of movement. Whereas I have to rearrange my entire world in order to step outside of my house alone. Why is that? Why does my life have to change so drastically while his changes very little? How is that fair? It's his kid too, is it not?

I know he works hard. It's not easy running your own company. I get that. I'm not mad that he works. I'm mad that it has become so much harder for me to have a semi-normal life yet for the father it's hardly changed at all. I don't recall deciding that I don't get to go anywhere from now on without Sammy.

Then, while sitting there in the dark, as I put Sammy on my other breast, it hit me. I never asked. I never told him. He must think everything is perfectly fine because I never told him otherwise. I never asked for a semi-normal life. But he did. He makes shit happen. Is this who I am now? I can't possibly have turned into a person who just waits for someone else to give a shit on her behalf. I wish I knew why I can't advocate for myself and express my own needs. I allow myself to suffer in silence—giving in to the years and years that my foremothers did the same, a sort of ancestral muscle memory. This doesn't help anyone. It just causes a lot of resentment on my part. Well, if he gets to do things outside the home without a baby and diaper bag and stroller in tow, then so do I.

You might think that this would be the moment where I placed Sammy back in his crib, walked across the hall to our bed where Kasim was enjoying a good read, and told him that from now on, I was going to leave the house every Saturday morning and he would watch the kid, because it's his kid too, dammit.

Alas, I think you know by now that that's not what I did.

This thought, this epiphany, didn't empower me like I thought it would. It weighed me down. The depression cloud was about to burst. It was as noticeable and as obvious as the weather man watching it storm outside and reporting a 100 percent chance of rain. Now I was aware more than ever of my caged existence and I wanted to break free, even if for a few moments. But I couldn't move.

The next day was a hard one. I moved because I had to. I smiled at Sammy because it was what he needed, not because I wanted to. I somehow managed to make it to the end of the day. Sammy was soundly asleep in his crib when Kasim came home from work. I was on the couch again, watching *Friends* on my iPad yet again. I didn't have the energy to cry but somehow I managed to produce tears, anyway.

Kasim came over and softly sat down on the edge of the couch. I could sense something in the air. Something uncomfortable between us. I didn't want to look at him. And I could tell he didn't want to talk to me.

"Are you okay?" He seems to always ask this question. Oddly enough it usually happens to be when I'm watching *Friends*. And I never give the answer he's looking for.

"I'm just tired. Sammy refused to nap, so I drove him around in the car until he fell asleep. But then when I put him in his crib he woke up. I tried to leave him there, let him cry it out, but he cried so hard he threw up. A lot. So I just wore him instead and cleaned while he slept on my chest. It was horribly uncomfortable. And it just pissed me off. I fucking hate this."

He sighed. That sigh rang out into the ether, making the silence stronger. Silence is scary to my little soul. I still wouldn't look him in the face. My anger still seemed directed at him as it was last night. It was like this switch was hit, and suddenly, instead of blaming Sammy for all of my woes, Kasim was to blame. It wasn't Sammy's fault that I was sad. It was Kasim's. He's the one who is never here. He is the one that has left me alone to take care of a child when I am completely inept. He's the one that continues to have a normal life. He's the one that is thriving with his work, writing books, and becoming, as I like to call it, "nerd famous." He's the one everyone loves. And I have become a no one. I am invisible. I have been forgotten. I am now just a mother. And there can be nothing worse.

I was fuming at this point, as I stared at the iPad that had timed out and turned into a black screen, projecting my angry reflection back at me. I should have just closed my eyes, pretending to fall asleep. But I couldn't perform. Not right now. I couldn't even do what I do best: avoid conflict at all costs. I wanted him to know. I wanted him to know that my life sucks, that he has no idea what I'm going through, that it's not fair that he gets to live a life that I want. But I didn't know how to put it into words. Every time I strung a combative sentence in my head, I instantly found a counterargument to my own point.

Kasim is smarter than I'll ever be. If I could easily dismantle my own thoughts, he could do it before I could even finish my point. Thinking of this only made me more angry. To know that I didn't know how to say what I felt, because what I felt was irrational, but made sense; stupid yet completely understandable; unfair, but right on the money. Kasim always tells me that I'm allowed to feel whatever it is that I'm feeling. That there is no wrong way. But here, in this moment, unable to explain myself because I don't understand anything that has happened, I'm just trapped in this giant hole, with no one around to hear me screaming, unable to get any help.

I was still waiting for him to speak. I wanted him to take the lead and I would just counterattack. But the silence continued, bringing with it a bout of anxiety. Anxiety makes me feel small. Like a puppy in need of care but with no idea of how to get it. Like a school child who is being punished for being bad. My internal moral compass gets thrown off. I can't figure out if I've done something wrong or if my ego is just taking over. Still, I could bear the silence no longer. Just as I was about to say something, mercifully, he spoke. I knew whatever was gonna come out of my mouth wasn't going to move the conversation in the proper direction. But then, the words he spoke made everything go sideways. Just four very simple words, and I became more muddled.

"What do you want?"

"What?" I quickly replied, looking at him for the first time.

"I don't know how to help you if I don't know what it is

that you want. So what is it that you want? Or maybe I should ask, 'What is it that you need?'" he responded with a stone-cold face.

Why was this such a hard question? Kasim would do anything he could to help his family. He solves problems for a living. And he's the most competent person I know. *Let him help. What do I want or need? Think, Suz. Think. What can help you get better?*

"I don't know," were the words that stumbled out of me.

Kasim sighed and got up, heading into the kitchen. I heard the sound of plates and silverware gently knocking around. He walked over to the dining table and set his plate of food down. I thought he was going to sit down and start eating. I was already looking forward to turning *Friends* back on. There was nowhere for this conversation to go, so why bother finishing it?

Instead of sitting down, he walked over to the living room and sat on the chair across from me. He stared at me for a few minutes before he began speaking. God, that was uncomfortable. Nothing had yet been said, but I began to cry softly. I was bracing myself for something I knew I wasn't going to be able to handle.

"I don't know what to do, Suz. I've tried everything I can think of. When I see that you're frustrated with Sam, I try to take him out to give you some time alone. I try to give you breaks on the weekend when I can see that it's too much for you.

"I have watched you tell anyone who will listen not to have a child. That they're crazy to think of having one. You've said on more than one occasion that if you could do it all over again, you wouldn't have had Sam. What am I supposed to do with that? It makes me not want to help you. Honestly, it makes me nervous to even leave you alone with the baby. Do you have any idea how many times I've worked from home just because I needed to keep an eye on you?"

I could tell he wanted to say more, but he stopped himself. Before he could let out another sound, he sealed his lips together and took a long, angry breath through his nose. He kept his eyes on me when he did. Hot tears were now pouring down my face as my entire body shook. I was looking at him like a little girl who is in trouble with a parent.

"Do you want to leave, Suz?"

"What?"

"You clearly don't want to be here. You don't want to be a mother. Do you want to leave? Just go away for a year until Sammy is more manageable? Go do whatever it is that Sammy is holding you back from and come back when you're ready. It's insane, but if that's what you want, if you want to go..."

For a millisecond, I let my mind consider that reality. I considered what it would be like to leave that little boy, with his big brown eyes that look just like mine, and his straight eyebrows that look just like Kasim's. I thought about the selfish life I would have, while Sammy spent this most important time without a mother. I couldn't finish the thought. Nothing in the world was more wrong. How could he think I would want that?

"Kasim," I whispered, barely able to hold myself up at this point. I leaned back against the couch, resting my head. I let out the kind of cry you let out when someone you love dies. I was mourning my life. I was, at that moment, mourning the person that I used to be. I was mourning for my marriage that seemed to be breaking. I was mourning for that little boy down the hall who needed a kind of love I was fighting hard to give but couldn't quite manage.

Kasim got up and came over to the couch and held my hand while I let this all out. After a few minutes, I pulled myself together, sat straight up, and looked right at him through blurry eyes. But then I couldn't do it, and looked down at my knees instead.

"Kasim," I repeated. "I'm not okay. I'm not okay at all. I'm depressed. And not like how we all casually throw around the word 'depressed.' I mean, I'm really, actually depressed. I've been doing some reading and talking to people who suffer from depression. And I'm pretty sure I have postpartum depression... and anxiety. Like having one of them isn't bad enough, I had to get both.

"When you first have a baby, it's normal to have a bit of postpartum issues—crying, sadness, body aches, anxiety, whatever. And I did. And I think it was completely normal. But then it never went away. And it only got worse. I've been trying so hard to fake it. At first I didn't know. I just thought that being a mom was the worst thing that can happen to a person. Then, after I realized that I'm probably depressed, I thought it would get better. I thought that now I've identified it, it's half the battle. But I just got angry and I was depressed that I was depressed.

"I love you. And I think I love Sammy. No, I know I love Sammy. I so desperately want to be a good mom for him. I look at him and it breaks my heart that I haven't been. He deserves better. And I wanna do better. I just get stuck in my head, and it's all consuming. My entire body is affected by it. I lose the ability to think straight, my mind goes down these horrific rabbit holes and I can't stop it. I'm sorry."

I was still staring at my knees, pretending to pick lint off of my pants. I did it. I told him. I had a horrible knot in my stomach, I was nauseated...my anxiety was making an appearance, right on schedule.

He put his hand under my chin and lifted my head to meet his gaze. He stared at me. He'd never looked at me that way before. I watched him look at my face, like he was trying to find the real Suz, like he almost found her. If he looked long enough, there she'd be. She was just waiting for someone to look, for someone to find her. His eyes grew larger.

"I had no idea. I really had no idea. I didn't know. I'm so sorry. I'm so sorry I didn't see it. It makes so much sense. This isn't you. You've never been this way before. How did I not realize something was going on? I'm so sorry."

"It's okay. I didn't know either. And when I did, I didn't know how to talk about it. I don't know why. I'm sorry I didn't tell you sooner. I'm not so good at advocating for myself. I should have told you."

Kasim pulled me into his chest. I clung to him like I was holding onto a life raft. I've never been a cuddler. It's always been a cute joke in our relationship. If there were two things he could change about me it would be that I was taller and a better cuddler. But here, in this moment, we weren't cuddling. We were grabbing onto our marriage, holding fast. I was relying on him to hold me up, just like he did when I was in labor. We had come full circle.

That cloud that was always following me around was being pushed away a little. It was still there. One moment of truth was not going to magically erase it. But it was a little further away, out of reach. I felt lighter but so very tired. Kasim leaned back onto the couch and I settled deeper into his embrace until I fell asleep.

After some time, I don't know how long, he picked me up, and laid me down in our bed.

"Kasim?" I asked as my head hit the pillow. "Is Sammy okay?" I thought I heard him crying. Part of being a new mother is that you always think you hear your baby crying for you, needing you.

"Yes, he's fine. I think he woke up. But I've got it. You get some rest."

"Thank you," I said, rolling over to get more comfortable.

"You're a good mother, Suzee," Kasim said as he stroked my hair.

"Thank you," I said again, half smiling. He wiped a tear from my face. Can you cry while you're sleeping?

SEPTEMBER 10, 2015:
A DO-OVER

"My love. My love, wake up." I heard Kasim's gentle voice next to me. I pulled the blanket over my head—the universal gesture for "Leave me alone, please." I wanted to keep sleeping. I slept so well last night. God, it felt good. I hadn't slept that well since before I was pregnant. I had so much sleep to catch up on.

But then I heard a soft little sound. A series of delightful gurgles. *Oh yeah, I have a kid to take care of. Of course I can't keep sleeping.*

"You have to get up now, lovebug. Sammy needs to eat." I pulled the blanket down and opened my eyes. There, in front of me, was my little world: my husband, to whom, just a few hours before, I had found my way back; and my child, who was the reason I had lost my way to begin with, or so I kept telling myself. But right now, they, both of them, made me smile. I lifted myself up into a seated position, ready to receive Sammy into my arms to begin nursing.

"I made you a cup of chai. Do you wanna sit on the patio while you feed him? It's not too hot outside," said Kasim.

"That sounds nice." He made me chai. It was a gesture. A

"we're in this together" sort of gesture. Quickly, I put all the pieces of last night together: Kasim carrying me to bed, then going to take care of Sammy when he woke up crying. He's taking care of me. Loving me in the ways I didn't know I needed him to. I threw the blankets off of me and got out of bed, my head pounding on all sides.

I went into the bathroom to brush my teeth while they headed off to the patio. I looked at myself in the mirror. I fell asleep before taking out my contacts. My eyes were dry and puffy. I took out my contacts and put on my glasses and tidied my hair a bit. *It's a new day. What happened last night was exactly what needed to happen. Count on him.*

When I made my way to the patio, I found my guys waiting for me, along with a steaming cup of chai next to the empty chair. I took a mental picture of Kasim smiling at our son, making silly faces. *What a beautiful thing.* I sat down and took a sip of my chai, savoring the smell and deep flavor and really appreciating that someone else had lovingly made it for me. My breasts were engorged. I had missed my middle of the night feeding. After Sammy was on my breast, I sighed in relief, the discomfort slowly leaving my chest. I picked up my cup and we all sat there together.

The energy around us was different. I didn't know how bad it was between Kasim and me until I no longer felt it. Whatever *it* was. Today was nothing like yesterday. I looked up at Kasim, purposely making eye contact. *Be brave today. He's on your side. He loves you.*

"Thank you, habibi," I said, smiling at him. "Thank you for feeding Sammy in the middle of the night or whatever time that was. I had no idea how much I needed uninterrupted sleep."

"Of course, lovebug." I watched him formulate his thoughts. It's not that I didn't want to talk, I was just drained. And if I'm being honest, I wanted to know what he thought about last night. Then he began.

"I'm really sorry, my love. I hate that you've been going through this alone. I should have known something was up. I was quick to get angry and didn't consider that you might be going through something.

"I keep thinking about how obvious it is now that I know. You never used to just burst out crying. Between the two of us, I'm the crier, not you. And to think that you blamed Sammy, a baby, for the state of your sadness just never made any sense. How did I not suspect anything? Why didn't I ask you? My God, why didn't I Google it?!"

Before I responded, I sipped my chai and sat in the silence contemplating a couple of things I was feeling:

Sympathetic: He must feel shitty knowing that his wife was suffering in silence. He would take on that responsibility and guilt and I didn't want him to do that.

Pissed: Now that he had mentioned it, why was he so quick to assume the worst? Why didn't he ask me if something was wrong? And for the love of God, he Googles everything. Why didn't he Google "My wife is acting crazy post baby"? Yes, he occasionally asked me if I was okay, but it's the kind of "Are you okay?" that anyone asks anyone who looks sad. Why was he so quick to just get angry at my response to motherhood instead of giving me the benefit of the doubt?

All of the good work we managed last night was unraveling as I kept asking myself these questions. When I looked back over at him, every angry thought dissipated. He was still looking at me and his eyes were filled with tears. My heart sank. He was a first-time parent too. He had to take care of me and this baby. And his partner was flailing but he didn't know why. And then a memory:

"I have to take care of you now." He spoke those words to me just over four years ago, days after our wedding. And my God, did he mean it. It was everything to him to take care of his family—as long as I give him the chance to.

With tears in my eyes, I grabbed his hand. "Hey, it's okay. All of this is new. Neither of us knows what we're doing. You've never been a parent before either. It's really hard!" I said the last line in my playful, slightly squeaky voice so he knew I was okay. I started to wonder about what happens to a man after becoming a father. Everything is about the mom and baby. And for the most part, it should be. But fathers are not just sperm donors. They too are changed by it all. They too worry for their child, wondering if they're doing right by them, feeling guilty for not seeing them as much as they would like. Dads have their own struggles. In time, I need to ask him. I need to see that he's okay too. We need to take care of each other.

"You wanna go to The Good Egg for breakfast?" Kasim asked as he cleared his throat.

"Don't you have to work? It's a Tuesday."

"I'm taking the day off. I wanna spend the day with you guys."

"Really? That's amazing. Thank you," I replied, truly touched by this gesture of love.

I finished my chai and nursing and went to get dressed while Kasim looked after Sammy. I chose to do something truly amazing this morning: I wore jeans, a casual but nice top, and a full face of makeup. This small act was revolutionary.

The three of us headed out to our favorite breakfast place: me, looking like a normal human, my handsome husband holding my hand, and our little baby, calm and laid back, who seemed to be feeding off of the energy of our morning.

Sammy fell asleep before we got to the restaurant. He sat in his car seat in the booth while we enjoyed a lovely morning of talking, laughing, and coming up with movie ideas (a favorite creative pastime of ours).

At the end of our lovely day, with Sammy in bed, Kasim and I plopped ourselves down on the couch.

"I had a really nice day," I said uncomfortably, allowing myself to be open and vulnerable.

"So did I."

Kasim put his hand on my cheek and looked into my eyes. Unlike the night before, he found a bit of his wife in there. While I'm glad he saw a part of the old me, I'm still horribly uncomfortable with long eye contact. How much does one need to stare into the eyes of another? This isn't a 1930s movie. To cut this horror short, I leaned in for a kiss. And though I say "lean," it was more of a pounce. Last night we had a beautiful and tender moment, but tonight, I needed something physical. I didn't want to be a woman struggling with her role as a mother, fighting depression. Right then, I needed to just be a woman, to be his wife. And his wife needed to feel wanted, needed to feel a basic carnal touch of a man.

I'd forgotten I was a woman. Tonight, he helped me remember.

OCTOBER 2, 2015:
COME AGAIN?

"Here. Drink water." Kasim handed me a glass of water as I choked on a bit of carrot.

"Are you okay?" he asked for the sixth time as I took slow, shallow breaths.

"Yeah. Yeah, I think I'm okay. Thank you," I said as I started to settle down and could finally get words out.

"What happened?"

"Well, let's see," I began somewhat obnoxiously. "Here we are, having a nice dinner, and out of the blue you mentioned a second baby. Are you crazy?"

"No. I'm not crazy. I don't think we ever talked about Sammy being an only child."

"I can barely handle the one we have. I'm a mess. How am I supposed to do this again?"

"I don't know. I'm not saying we decide right now. But we really should start to think about it. If we did have another kid, I think they should be close in age so they grow up together and can be best friends."

"You're just trying to recreate your childhood with your brother," I said, drinking more water and not daring to eat any food.

"Maybe. I don't know. But I do know that life as an only child is a lonely one. And I don't want that for Sammy."

It was then that I looked over at Sammy. He was playing in his little office that my godmother gave me at my baby shower. He was old enough now to sit in it and enjoy being surrounded by stimulating toys. I watched him play and wondered what his Christmases would be like without any siblings to share them with. No one to spy on Santa with in the middle of the night. No one to rip open presents with. No one to play jokes on at bedtime.

I started to think of my own childhood with my own siblings. When you're the oldest of four and have immigrant parents, so much responsibility falls to you. There were so many times that I didn't get to just be a child, one of the kids. I had to take charge and be my mom's right hand man. Right hand maid. A sous-mother, if you will. I had a sudden thought of how much I must have helped her if she had to go through this with my younger siblings. Sandy's intellectual disability was a heavy burden on my mom, a young twenty-three-year-old mother whose husband worked fourteen-hour days. Not to mention, my brother had more energy than a baby German shepherd, and Selwa embodied every exhausting, stereotypical characteristic of the baby in the family.

I started to smile. As crazy as it was having to be a caretaker in my family, I was wonderfully happy. I had a good childhood, I was well taken care of, and I had built-in company in my siblings. We were never apart. Our holidays were loud and chaotic. I didn't realize how much I miss that. The noise. The dozen or so shoes at the front door that indicated a house full of people. What a beautiful thing.

"Yeah. I don't want that for Sammy, either. But I can't talk about this right now. It's too much. Is that okay? We're in a good place, you and I. And I'm not trying to shut you out. I just really can't talk about it. I can sense my body starting to react negatively. I'm just not ready."

"Sure. Yeah. That's fine. I should have thought that through. I was just talking out loud. I didn't mean to force you into anything," Kasim gently said as he took my hand. "I love you."

"I love you, too. And thank you."

But it was too late. It was happening. As much as I loved those memories of me and my siblings, still, it was happening; the heaviness, the negative thoughts were creeping in. *How on earth could I do this again? I won't survive it.*

"You know what, uh, I think I'm gonna go take a shower. You got Sammy?"

"Yup. Go ahead."

I got up and walked straight past Sammy, without looking down at him. In the shower, I sat on the floor with my knees to my chest. *It's too hard. I can't do it again. I won't survive it. I can't do it. It's too hard.*

It's too hard. I don't know if I can do it. I wish someone could tell me what to do.

OCTOBER 31, 2015:
THE HEART OF A LION

"It's too big."

"Well, he's just so tiny," I replied to Kasim as I watched him put a lion costume on Sammy. "It looks more like the lion ate Sammy."

Kasim laughed. I love when I can make him laugh. It's like having a superpower. Making funny people laugh isn't easy. Comedians have high standards for funny.

"He still looks cute, though."

"That's because Sammy is just a cute baby," I said. Postpartum depression or not, there's no denying that he's a cute kid. I'm just being objective here.

Today, we took Sammy to Modern Milk for a little Halloween party. I have been going to Modern Milk for a few months now and it's my safe space, my refuge when I can't stand another minute at home and need a baby-friendly, and mom-friendly, place to go. To be.

I've been getting stronger as I take barre there a few days a week. Though if I'm honest, I haven't been going as much as I'd like to. I have the time and Lord knows I'm bloody bored. But some days, as much as I'm dying to leave the house, to see other human beings, I can't move. I just feel like a zombie who has been stunned by a stunning charm.

Opening up to Kasim last month changed everything. My postpartum depression and anxiety haven't gone away, but Kasim is starting to notice the signs and he jumps to my aid, gladly.

"What do you need right now?" he'll ask when he sees me sitting there with my eyes slightly out of focus, staring off into some unknowable fourth dimension.

"I'm tired," I might say.

"Does Sammy need to be fed?"

"No. I just nursed him."

"Then go take a nap. I'll wake you up in an hour or so."

I'll nod and drag myself to bed. I'll open the curtains to let in as much light as I can. And I'll fall asleep with a few rays of light shining on me, wrapping around me like a blanket. A bit of warmth and love and happiness in those beams of light.

Kasim worked from home today since your kid's first Halloween is a big deal.

When we walked into Modern Milk, I felt as if I was the owner, proud to show Kasim this fine establishment that I love so much.

I hated it.

Modern Milk is a unique concept. There's nothing like it in all the land. And dammit, every new mother knew it. While that's great for their business, it was terrible for me.

We were surrounded. Surrounded by tiny, sweet monsters,

vampires, Hilarys and Trumps, pumpkins…It wasn't the baby creatures that bothered me. It was the amount of people. *I thought I loved people?*

"Hey, Suz!" My new Modern Milk mama friend, Flavia, with her child Jacob (today he was a construction worker) in tow, waved us over to her. We squeezed through the clusters of parents and infants to greet her.

"Hey, Flavia, how are you?" I asked, hugging and kissing my Swiss Italian friend as European custom dictates. "This is Kasim. K, this is Flavia and Jacob."

"It's nice to meet you," they both said simultaneously while shaking hands as American custom dictates.

We then exchanged our usual, "Your kid looks so cute… getting so big…yes, it seems like he's regressed in his sleeping patterns…oh, he's finally tried solid foods…."

"It's crowded in here," I confessed to my friend and my husband. "I don't like it."

"It's never bothered you before," Kasim replied.

"I know. I usually love being around loads of people. But I really hate this."

"Do you wanna go?"

"Yeah, actually, I do. Is that okay? There's not even a place to sit down for Sammy to enjoy story time."

"Wait!" Flavia cried out. "Can we at least go into the barre room and just take pictures of our boys. They look so cute."

We snuck into the studio and snapped photos of our confused children. As long as I was in this room, I was okay.

What is happening? I suddenly turned into an old person who doesn't like noises and crowds. Is this normal?

When we got back in the car I took a really long and deep breath.

"Are you okay?" Kasim asked yet again. But this "are you okay" was different. I knew he was genuinely asking and wanted to help.

"Yeah, I'm good. It's strange, but I couldn't breathe in there. I don't know why. I was internally freaking out. It was just too many people and I had this weird instinct of wanting to protect Sammy from the crowd. It doesn't make any sense, but there it is."

Kasim smiled.

"What's so funny? I just admitted to being an agoraphobe. That's not funny.

"It's not that. Can I speak honestly?"

"That's a stupid question, of course you can." Kasim raised his eyebrow at me and said nothing. "Okay. Sorry. Not a stupid question. Honesty scares me. But yes, go ahead."

"It just made me happy to hear that you instinctively wanted to protect Sammy. I know you've had a hard time adjusting to motherhood. But I can see that you love him. And after all the times I've heard you say that you wish this was all a dream, it's been nice to watch you open up more to him."

"I have?"

"Yeah. I've been watching you guys. And you're different now. I'm not saying whatever you're going through has vanished, but you don't seem to hold Sammy responsible anymore."

"Hm," was all I could get out.

I love him. I looked back at Sammy in his car seat. His lion costume was thrown next to him. He seemed happy with our morning out and he was babbling away in gratitude. I looked at him with a stupid smile on my face. Even though I couldn't see my own face, I recognized the spirit of that smile. It's the way every mom looks at her child. With that inexplicable love that comes shooting out from your stomach, where his life began, where you first connected to him, where you will always be connected to him.

A tear fell from my face before I noticed that I was moved by this revelation. I'm depressed for the first time in my life, my anxiety is worse than it has ever been, but I'm changing. I'm learning to love him the way I thought I was supposed to from the start but just couldn't. I'm learning that Sammy coming into my life isn't the end of anything but the beginning of a different kind of life.

And I get to decide how to shape it.

EPILOGUE

Time is relative. But for the sake of this story, I'll just say, as much as it annoys me, time only moves forward. And so, time went on.

AUGUST 6, 2021:
A NEW CHAPTER

"Hurry up! We're late!" I yelled out to Sammy and Ronan. "I don't wanna go to school. It's not fun!" Sammy yelled out.

"Sammy, habibi, don't talk like that in front of your brother. It's his first time at school and you shouldn't say anything that will make him not want to go."

"I don't want to go to school either, Mama!" Ronan shouted as he ran toward Sammy and me with no clothes on.

"Ronan! Why aren't you dressed yet? We're late!"

"I can't do it."

"My love, you're four years old. You're a big boy now. I won't do anything for you that you can do yourself," I tried to say calmly as I held Ronan's hand and walked him back to his room.

"Mama! The pancakes smell bad!" I heard Sammy shout from the kitchen.

"God dammit!" I muttered as I ran back to the kitchen to flip the burning pancakes.

"God dammit! God dammit!" Ronan parroted throughout the house, still naked.

It was a bad start to the first day of school.

"What's that smell?" Kasim inquired a few minutes later as he walked into the kitchen ready and dressed for the day.

"It's the smell of chaos. Welcome to the first day of school," I sarcastically replied.

"It's okay, lovebug. I'll help you get them ready. Just think about it. You've been waiting for this day. The boys are both in school full time now. You get your life back."

"I know. I can't believe it. I haven't been alone for over six years. It's gonna be amazing. And weird. But mostly amazing." I sipped my coffee and tried to imagine a clean house. A quiet house.

"Let's drop them off together then go get coffee," Kasim suggested.

"Oh my God we can do that, can't we? Just get up and go get coffee without having to figure out what to do with the kids? I can't compute that." I was stunned.

Kasim helped Sammy and Ronan to finish getting ready while I wrapped up in the kitchen, cleaning up breakfast and making school lunches.

"Off we go!" I said excitedly, ushering everyone out of the door.

As we buckled the boys into the back seat I felt things shifting in my life. *Just a few more minutes and that's it. I'm free.*

As Kasim drove, I looked back at both of my boys. My eyes settled on Ronan for a moment. This was his first day of school. It was a big moment. *How did I get so lucky to have him?* While Sammy has darker skin, beautiful big brown eyes, and thick dark hair, Ronan is his antithesis. I smiled at him while I looked him over before we pulled into his school; I took in his blue-green eyes, his white skin, and his dirty-blond hair. I made myself laugh thinking of how many people have asked me if the boys have the same father when they look so different.

"Nope. I'm just lucky," I would reply to these rude, idiot strangers.

"Okay boys, we're here," Kasim's voice snapped me back to the present moment.

A teacher walked up to open the car door and helped the boys out of the car.

"Bye, Mama! Bye, Daddy! I love you! Bye!" Both Sammy and Ronan said on repeat.

"We love you so much, habibi. Bye!" I responded, getting choked up.

They turned and walked away from the car. I couldn't take my eyes off the back of their little round heads. "Are you okay?" Kasim asked, grabbing my hand.

"Wait! Don't drive away yet." I jumped out of the car and ran toward them. I hugged them, held them, and cried. "I'm so proud of you two. I love you so much."

I pulled back and looked at Sammy square in the eyes. A moment of grief passed through my body as I remembered that at one point in my life I regretted that he was born. Yet now, I love him so much I can't stand it. It's indescribable.

The teacher gently pulled them away and they both said goodbye one more time.

"I thought you'd be celebrating right now," Kasim said while I buckled myself back in the car, wiping tears from my face.

"No. This is good."

"What's good? That you're sad?"

"Yes. I'm glad I'm sad. I spent so much time wishing they weren't here, wishing I wasn't a mother, wanting space from them. I can't tell you how happy it makes me that I'm sad to see them head off to school. It means I love them."

"Of course you love them. You're a good mother."

"I didn't always feel like I loved them. I didn't always feel like a good mother. This moment of sadness is a reminder of that; of where I was and where I am."

Kasim smiled. "It was just you and the boys for so long. It's the end of an era."

I could feel it. I could feel one chapter of my life closing and a new one beginning. I made it through.

ACKNOWLEDGMENTS

A very big thank you to my husband, Kasim Aslam, for reading and rereading and for holding my hand through it all.

Thank you to Jackie Cangro for your editing brilliance and insight.

Susan Balk, thank you for being my sounding board at the beginning.

To Nancy Aslam, my mother-in-law, who kept me sane.

To Nadine Saad and Sandra Lemenaite, thank you for listening in the darkness.

AUTHOR NOTE

When my friends ask me for advice on a matter, I get nervous. What if it's the wrong advice? What if the words aren't comforting enough? So I've taken to lending an ear and making them laugh. In a book, I cannot lend you my ear, but I can lend you my thoughts. And maybe you'll find some of those thoughts funny. And maybe you'll laugh.

I'm not offering advice or a cure. Motherhood is sisterhood. And the thing about a sisterhood that is so appealing is that you don't feel alone. You have comrades to hold you up, to support you, to take over when you need a break. I think I would have felt better if I knew I wasn't alone in my struggles or dark thoughts, that I wasn't actually a bad person.

And that's why I wrote *Postpardon Me*. To be with you, to hold you up, to show support, and to give you a little break should you need it.

Being a mother is hard- with each passing phase, a new one presents itself bringing along a new set of challenges. But you figure things out, you learn to ask for help, you stop being hard on yourself and you pick up tools along the way.

Above all, you will see the connection that you share with

your child. You will see how you are actually the light of his life, how he will always forgive you when you mess up, how his love for you is so abundant that he teaches you how to take care of him, and how to be a better person.

ABOUT THE AUTHOR

Suzanne is a mother of two gorgeous little guys and can't remember what else she is. Oh yes, she's been an activist, an actor and former Miss Arab USA. Suzanne lives in Scottsdale, Arizona with said littles and her incredible husband, Kasim.

To learn more about Suzanne, please visit her website:

suzanneyatimaslam.com

You can also connet with her on Instagram:

www.instagram.com/suzyatimaslam